FOREWORD BY DONALD MILLER

FAITH OF MY FATHERS

Conversations with Three Generations of Pastors
about Church, Ministry, and Culture

ZONDERVAN

Chris Seay

FAITH OF MY FATHERS

Conversations with Three Generations of Pastors
about Church, Ministry, and Culture

by Chris Seay

GRAND RAPIDS, MICHIGAN 49530 USA

Faith of My Fathers: Conversations with Three Generations
of Pastors about Church, Ministry, and Culture
Copyright © 2005 by Chris Seay

Youth Specialties Products, 300 South Pierce Street, El Cajon, CA 92020, are published by
Zondervan, 5300 Patterson Avenue SE, Grand Rapids, MI 49530

Library of Congress Cataloging-in-Publication Data

Seay, Chris.
  Faith of my fathers : conversations with three generations of pastors
about church, ministry, and culture / by Chris Seay.
     p. cm.
  ISBN-10: 0-310-25326-8 (pbk.)
  ISBN-13: 978- 0-310-25326-6 (pbk.)
  1. Pastoral theology--Baptists--Miscellanea. 2. Seay, Chris--Family
--Miscellanea.   I. Title.
  BV4011.3.S43 2005
  286'.1'092273--dc22
  [B]   2005015115

Web site addresses listed in this book were current at the time of publication. Please contact
Youth Specialties via e-mail (YS@YouthSpecialties.com) to report URLs that are no longer
operational and replacement URLs if available.

Editorial direction by Donald Miller
Art direction by Holly Sharp & Chris Seay
Editing by Janie Wilkerson
Proofreading by Laura Gross and Joanne Heim
Cover and interior design by Holly Sharp
Printed in the United States

05 06 07 08 09 10 / DCI / 10 9 8 7 6 5 4 3 2 1

DEDICATION

I am Chris Seay.

I am a pastor, father, author, husband, storyteller, Astros fan, teacher, Texan, student, swimmer, theologian, film critic, spiritual guide, former bed-wetter, lifeguard, artist, Continental One Pass Gold Elite Member, Baylor Bear, referee, singer, instigator, and Houstonian.

But from my first breath I have always been a **son.**

This book is dedicated to my fathers and mothers:

Betty Baldwin (a.k.a. Noni)—Out of the ashes of a challenging family of origin, you nurtured our family to be what it is today. Your love of the church, Scripture, family, and "the least of these" has not gone unnoticed. I love you!

Robert Baldwin (a.k.a. Papa or Brother Bob)—You are the most powerful and loving man I have ever known. I have the hardest time imagining life without you—please listen to Dr. Bacak and stop eating sugar and fried food. I need you!

Ed Seay (a.k.a. Dad)—There is no one on the planet whom I respect more than you. You embody the best of what it means to be a father and a pastor. The greatest compliment I can receive is when people say, "You are so much like your dad."

Cindy Seay (a.k.a. Mom)—Thank you for being stronger than anyone anticipated, for never getting stale, and for pursuing truth and loving others even when you knew it would hurt you. Your life is a story of the power of faith. I cannot describe my gratitude. More than anyone else, you have intimately shared the most important days in my life.

ACKNOWLEDGEMENTS

Chris:
This book is a collective work—a labor of love by everyone involved, including:

Blake Mathews—thanks for all your hard work transcribing these conversations and helping to pull things together.

Tyndall Wakeham—it is so great to work with you in every arena of my life. Thanks for helping us tell this story visually.

Donald Miller—you are a true friend and my favorite writer. It has been so much fun having your skilled hand helping me to shape this book. Thank you!

To everyone at Zondervan and YS—I couldn't be more grateful for your creativity, skill, and patience with this project. Special thanks to Jay, Marko, Holly, Roni, and John Raymond.

Thanks to Greg Garrett, Baylor University, my Baptist Family (especially UBA and BGCT), Acts 29, The Houstonian, Tia Marias, The Bisagno's, and the Houston Astro's.

To my beloved friends the Saharawi, including Steve and Lily—I pray every day that you will return to your homeland. I am blessed by your perseverance and passionate love of life.

To the elders, deacons, and entire church of WEBC and Ecclesia—I am so blessed to do the work of the gospel with you.

To my entire family—I thank you and love you from the bottom of my heart. The most frustrating part of this book is that the readers only get to know some of the pastors in my family. You are all amazing people and I am so proud of you. I especially want to thank my two beautiful sisters, Jennifer and Jessica.

Lisa—you are the love of my life, my partner, and friend. Thanks for allowing me the time to pursue this project.

Hanna, Trinity, and Solomon—my greatest dream is to someday share similar conversations with you all and your children.

Papa:
To write about my family and how they are being used in the Lord's work and how God is using them is a joy. But I must begin with the first woman in my life, for without her it would be impossible for me to be where I am today. I am fully convinced that, apart from the Lord, there is no one as responsible for the success of our family as my wife, Betty. She is responsible for any success I may have had in the ministry; she is my love and my friend. Even after all these years, her wisdom, judgment, and leadership continue to amaze me. Her love for Christ has shown our children what it means to live for him in every situation of life.

Ed:
In reflecting on the faith that draws our family together, I feel compelled to acknowledge three women in our family whose influence could never be overstated:

My grandmother, Winnie Corine Standley (a.k.a. Granny), who undertook the daunting tasks of raising her grandson and imparting to him her own faith in Christ in a way that has shaped every facet of his life.

Betty Baldwin, whose quiet spiritual strength and sacrificial love for her Lord and her family continues to demonstrate grace to us all.

Cindy Seay, my wife and best friend. She is the most gifted and spiritual individual I have ever known. What the Lord has done in the lives of our children is due, in no small measure, to the example and leadership of this incredible woman. How blessed I am that she is my partner in ministry and in life.

Without these three godly mothers, the "faith of our fathers" could never have had the impact on our children that it has.

Brian:
I would like to thank Amy—for always being there and pushing me to be a better husband, father, and friend.

Olivia, Phillip, Natalie, and Nathaniel—you guys constantly put life into perspective for me. Your hugs, smiles, and laughs are irreplaceable—I love you!

Dad and Mom—thanks for living out the words you say and thanks for letting us be ourselves and not some form of ourselves that fit someone else's expectations.

Chris, Lisa, Hanna, Trinity, Solomon, Jenn, Rusty, Emma, Jax, Justus, Rob, Liz, Ethan, Eliana, Jess, Shaun, Becky, Gabriella, Gresham, Penelope, Kathy, Phil, and Brenda (wow! that's a big family)—thanks for making family something to look forward to and not just endure.

Noni and Papa—your love and legacy of faith live on in an entire family and will continue to be felt for generations to come.

Thanks to Meadowbrook, Lake Limestone, First Baptist Church of Amarillo, IKON at The People's Church, and Mosaic Austin— the experiences, good and bad, have helped me to realize what it truly means to follow Jesus.

Robbie:
Liz, Ethan, Eliana—my love and thoughts are always with you. I love you with all that is within me.

Papa, Dad, Chris, Brian—you guys have shown me that being a man is more than American machoism crap—it means loving God, loving my family, admitting when I'm an idiot, and learning to hold on tight when life begins to whirl you around. For that—thank you.

Dan, Ryan, Chase, Chad K., Ecclesia, and our EMI family—with love and blessings, I thank God for all of you.

TABLE OF CONTENTS

TABLE OF CONTENTS

FOREWORD

During the summer of 2004, I lived for a bit in the small apartment above Chris Seay's garage. He and his family live on a golf course just north of downtown Houston, and I would wake to look out the window and through the humidity at the fifth tee, while golfers—at ungodly hours of the morning—smacked a little white ball across the length of Chris's backyard toward a green encircled by once-posh mansions, the owners of which had long ago moved further out and left the settlement to new families attempting to revitalize an area speckled in the cancer of their parents' strip malls.

The Seays are progressive. Lisa made fruit concoctions for me in the morning, all the contents of which were descended from the products one might find at the local market 4,000 years ago in the Garden of Eden. "White flour is the same stuff they use to hang wallpaper," she told me. "The preservatives in most foods will kill you," she went on to explain. She and Chris live incredibly healthy lives, Chris going so far as to get biannual colonics, which involves going to a naturopath and having a water hose shoved up your anus. "You wouldn't believe the stuff that gets lodged in your bowels," he said to me one afternoon while driving to Taft Street Coffee, the coffee shop and bookstore that he and his church own and operate in Montrose, the heart of the gay district in Houston.

We hung out at the shop for a few hours. Chris took me through the art gallery, then upstairs to the recording studio, and then next door to the old church. The pews had been removed to build a large living space, not unlike the set of MTV's *Real World*, to house theology students and artists and whoever else wants to live in intentional community. I have to tell you, I was impressed. I didn't know there were any progressive thinkers in Texas. I thought they'd all moved to San Francisco. And I certainly didn't expect a southern pastor—the never-changing, cloned role model for the would-be traditional Right—to own a coffee shop, or for that matter an art gallery, or for that matter to agree to have a water hose shoved up his anus and talk about it openly. But here he was. And I confess I wondered where he had come from, what hippie parents had raised him in what commune, and how he got all the way down here to Texas where the Karma is less thick with his own color.

But it was later that evening when I saw another side of Chris. We had dinner at a little Asian place in the shadow of the skyscrapers—tofu juiced up to taste like chicken—and then we went over to the hospital to visit a woman from Chris's congregation. It was late but Chris knew, because of her surgery schedule, that she would be up and lonely. We walked through the long corridors as Chris explained that his young, progressive congregation had recently melded with an ancient church in the city, one that was dying—literally—its few remaining parishioners dotting the sea of brown pews with their gray-blue hair, their brown suits with burgundy ties, their bald heads, their outdated opinions, their traditional demands, the years so thick on their hands they wrinkle on the palms. Chris talked about these people as though they were friends, no different than the hippies at the coffee shop.

As we tapped gingerly on the woman's door, I saw a side of Chris I could never have imagined. He greeted the woman with a kiss on the forehead, and she placed her palm, the skin of which seemed to double itself on the crooked bone of her hand, along his face and rubbed down to his beard. My friend was not just a progressive thinker or a postmodern leader—he was a pastor. He was *her* pastor. She spoke softly about the surgery, careful to let him in on every detail, and he never took his eyes out of her eyes, stroking back her thin gray hair and lightly setting her head against the pillow. He leaned in on the rail and nodded yes to her as she hoped out loud that the doctors had dealt directly with the problem. He talked to her about God being with her during each step, and even now in the recovery stage, even now as her body began to heal of the roughness of the knife. The woman found comfort in Chris; she found Christ in Chris. She found faith, belief, love, community, a Shepherd, a leader—dare I say, a *father*—a physician, all of these things—a pastor. My friend was a pastor.

I asked Chris about it on the way home. I asked him where he learned the confidence to stand in authority next to a woman three times his age and counsel her in the comfort and truth of God. That is when Chris explained to me that his father was a pastor and his father before him; he comes from a family of pastors. "It's the family business," he said, "though there isn't any money in it. God called my line to this—to shepherd people into faith; to believe ourselves, then invite others to believe; to represent God, his love, his kindness. And I learned it from my fathers. I learned faith from the ones who went before me."

I spent the next several months attending Chris's church, meeting with his father and his grandfather, watching as Chris mined his family for the knowledge that went into this book. They are not like him in many ways, and his father is as different from Chris as he himself is different from his father before him. They are different men, created by different generations, each with a language and a style and an understanding of worship and community and social justice. But in a way, what they have passed down to each other is identical; they have passed the love of God and the responsibility to communicate that love to a hurting world. They stand in miraculous confidence that this is precisely what God would have them do.

The beauty of this story—of what you are about to read—lies in its subtlety. This isn't a self-help book. If anything, it is a documentary. And I hope it is a documentary that gives you a glimpse through a window and into a family that has dedicated itself to this role of pastoring—a lost art that survives change, shifts in culture, even shifts in fashion. I came to Houston believing that the most important people in a society are legislators, businessmen, and athletes. But I left there convinced that the most important people in society are pastors. God bless them. God bless you.

Donald Miller

CHAPTER 1

SOME INTRODUCTIONS

How a Pastor Becomes a Pastor and Why

The book you are about to read has taken many forms during the development stages and throughout the creative process. The original plan was to take my grandfather, father, and brothers on an RV trip to important places in our ministry heritage and record our stories, conversations, and theological debates. This chronicle would then offer a model for complex-yet-loving relationships in the midst of passionate disagreement.

You see, the church in North America is in danger of self-destruction. The world has exploded with change over the last 50 years, and the church has been ill prepared for it. Either we will embrace our missional identity and thrive, or we will pick one another apart in the ensuing frustration. The same reality is true in my family; with three generations of pastors, we embody the present tension of the church. In so many ways, we are radically different from each other, but at the same time we share a deep love and respect for one another that ties us together. If we can love one another, compromise, and choose love over dogma—the rest of the church can do the same.

My grandfather suffered a heart attack before we could leave on our RV trip. He is doing well now, but we all thought it best not to travel. So as fate would have it, I am writing the book that decent people would wait their entire lives to write. A person's perspective can change, and it might have been better for me to wait until I am older and able to look back at the differing paradigms through the cleaner lens of hindsight. But in doing so, something would have been lost, and that something is the present tension.

The ache in the church is felt right now in my family. My grandfather was a different kind of pastor from my father, and I am yet a different kind of pastor. We disagree quite passionately, and yet we have no choice but to love and respect each other. We are not strangers who can easily be reduced to enemies and ignored. We are each other's sons, sharing each other's blood, needing each other's affection. And so we stay, and we listen, and we attempt to understand. How I wish for something as beautiful for the church as a whole. Through the blood of Christ, we are each other's sons and daughters as well, and we can't walk away from this responsibility any longer.

In this book my fathers paint the world and their families—and most of all, themselves—as they really are. I write this book at age 32 because Anne Lamott has taught me that embracing people as they are and writing about it may be the truest form of love. God, the Author of the Scriptures, told the story just as it was. The Book is compelling because the human beings in it are unsavory characters who appear to belong more in a bar or in a prison than in a church. And if this is the methodology God chose to tell his story, I have to borrow from its power to tell my own. I have not written a puff piece about my family. I love these men, but you will not be well served unless I tell you the whole story. My family and I wanted to have a frank and open conversation in the hopes that people could learn something from the unique petri dish that is our family—a family for whom I am grateful.

My brother Robbie Seay wrote a song that we sing at Ecclesia, and it arose from our discussions surrounding this book:

We are not alone
We did not begin here
Standing on your own
You are not forgotten
To all who've gone before, to all who've gone before
We are crying...thank you.

This is our faith, faith of our fathers
Faith of all martyrs
This is our faith, faith of believers, faith of believers
This is our faith.

Robbie is right; I have inherited the faith of my fathers and mothers, so I seek to tell our stories. Moses was a grandson of Abraham, and I imagine he was often embarrassed to write down the tales of his grandfather. Will history judge him harshly? Like a coward, he kept pimping out his wife and making money from it. He also sent his firstborn son into the desert to die. I hardly like the guy—the only guy I hate more is his so-called "righteous" nephew Lot who offered his daughters to a bunch of angry men to be gang-raped. If I see that guy in heaven, I promise I'll poke him in the eye. Yet Moses never censored the stories, and the end result told a story of faith that is attainable: imperfect people being loved by a perfect God.

Ironically, the church and Christian subculture want the sanitized version of everything. If you want a sanitized version of the human story, you have to look at Christ and Christ alone. The rest of us are sinners stumbling our way through the wreckage of the Fall. So in this book we are going to be honest with you about the changing face of life in ministry.

INTRODUCTIONS

Let me introduce you to the men who will bare their souls:

My grandfather Robert Steele Baldwin (Papa) left a series of offbeat jobs, such as driving a Twinkie truck and selling vacuum cleaners at Sears, to become an evangelist and eventually the pastor of Mangum Oaks Baptist Church in Houston. Mangum Oaks was a fledgling congregation with fewer than 10 people in 1966, but the church began to explode in the coming years. My grandfather, a gifted orator, told the story of faith with passion and biblical conviction. In the midst of this steady growth, the church relocated to new facilities in a thriving area just outside Houston's 610 loop and added staff members. One of the new hires was my father, **Edgar Martin Seay**, a young college-student-turned-music-minister who quickly began to fancy the 16-year-old daughter of his new boss and who courageously married this teenage girl. In 1971, she gave birth to me, **James Christopher Seay**.

This is my heritage. It is where I come from. And despite the radical difference of my own ministry and lifestyle, I think of this brand of faith, which I'll call "Revivalist Baptist," as the epicenter of my faith journey. At times I long for the security and nostalgia of that distant land. I feel like Abraham—all at once loving this new adventure, but missing the tranquility of my homeland. One can often find me wandering the grounds of my grandfather's old church where he preached his fiery sermons calling all to repentance and baptized dozens each week. I even uncovered the old baptismal robe he wore as he baptized hundreds of men, women, and children, and then gave it to him for Christmas last year as a symbol of my respect for his faithful service to God.

Mangum Oaks Baptist Church represents the homeland to me. It is a Mecca to all that it means to be Revivalist. Yet the church no longer exists; it has been swallowed by the emerging post-Christian urban landscape. This formerly thriving church, which my grandfather pastored for 28 years, held its last service in the church's 75,000-square-foot home in 2002. And for me, it feels like there is no homeland. Instead I make camp somewhere in the remnant of the shift and try to build a church. What happened? Where did the old church go? Did my grandfather's stories really happen? Why won't the same methodology work now?

That is what this book is about: people looking for a center, a home, and a tribe that will become a family. And like the Son of Man, we seek a place to lay our heads, theologically speaking. I need my grandfather and I need my father. I need them to tell me I'm doing okay, that I am shepherding people toward Christ, not just entertaining them. I need them in this great shift that is shaking the ground beneath my feet. I need them; I resent them; I love them; I am frustrated by them; I adore them.

I want God to give my congregation the stability that was so evident in their ministries. I am convinced God can and wants to. But how?

As Doug Pagitt says, "Revivalism is about re-igniting a latent faith that existed within people," and yet there seems to be no flame there to re-ignite. There seems to be no familiarity with the story of God and what he did in this city only 50 short years ago. All that is left is utter skepticism and a faint, dim-lit picture of a meta-narrative.

I am now post-revivalist. Within two generations, the religious landscape of America and my family has experienced a transmutation. Papa is the consummate 1950s evangelist, Dad is a Swindoll-esque pastor, and I thought I would lose my mind if I followed them into ministry. So I charted a new course and had no real idea where I was going. Thankfully, I embarked on this journey with their blessing. So now we come to the table—my father, my grandfather, and I—and I have questions. I am also wondering this: just as they have so much to teach me, do I have something to teach them? I wonder if they would be able to humble themselves before me, just as I humble myself before them, so we can learn from each other. Can I learn the importance of taking a stand against sin and depravity, if they can learn the importance and beauty of an inclusive community? I am wondering if they can learn the power of art and beauty as a necessary means of communicating to a whole human being, and I am wondering if I can learn more about the importance of propositional truth. There is a good chance we will be throwing dishes at each other before the thing is done. But I have hope.

My father and grandfather and I disagree, often vehemently, but they gave me this faith; and I believe the essentials (for example, the Apostles' Creed) haven't changed. I am wondering, though, if almost everything else is up for grabs.

Examining stories is my favorite pastime, but entering into my own story is a different thing altogether. I like to write about faith and popular culture because I love art and film and the subject is separate from my journey and requires very little introspection. Looking inside and searching is the most vital of spiritual exercises, yet it is the most challenging and painful. This journey to consider my life and ministry in the broader context of being a third-generation pastor is both life-giving and agonizing. I am honored to write this book, and at the same time I would rather have my legs broken than look deep into my soul and history. Journey with me as I consider the state of the church in North America through the lens of my own family.

Many believe the church in North America is headed toward extinction. But I possess great hope as I sit with these stories and the profound wisdom passed on from my father and grandfather. We want to invite you to eavesdrop on our conversations—but more than that, we want you to engage, to learn what we will learn, disagree as we will disagree, laugh as we will laugh, become angry as we become angry, and stay as we will not walk away. We simply need each other too much.

I don't always agree with my dad and grandfather, but I trust them more than anyone I could invent. Their collective stories are the well from which I draw wisdom during my periods of confusion. When life, family, or ministry drags me to the limits of my own sanity, their words always deliver hope to the part of my soul that's ready to give up.

We got together over at Papa's house, which is just a short throw from my father's house, in the woods north of Houston. My brothers, Robbie and Brian, came; and Papa, Dad, and I rounded the table. I also asked Don Miller, a family friend, to come and help guide a bit of the conversation from an outsider's perspective. Everybody already knew what I was up to: that I wanted to write our stories and mine their wisdom not just for my sake, but also for the church as a whole. We chose Papa's place because our wives could hang out at Dad's, letting the kids run around in the woods. There is great Mexican food in town, as in most small Texas towns, and I knew a healthy dose of carbohydrates for lunch might get us all feeling tired and vulnerable. Something pure might come to the surface, if not before lunch, then certainly after.

BEGINNINGS: PAPA'S EARLY YEARS

Here's how our first meeting went:

CHRIS: Hey Pop, would you pray for us, for our time?

PAPA: I will. Father, we want to thank you for the blessings that you share with us day in and day out, for the opportunity that we have as a family to worship you and to fellowship together as a family, but also to be together and fellowship in you. We ask you to guide and to direct and to bless us in everything that we say, in everything that is done today, that all that we do might only be for the purpose of lifting your name. We praise you and give you the glory for everything. We ask all these things in the name of Jesus, Amen.

CHRIS: Thanks, Papa. Well, thanks for agreeing to meet. I know you guys are busy. It was good of our wives to let us hang out and do this and watch the kids. Can we start out by taking a minute to introduce ourselves, in our own words? Dad, can we start with you?

DAD: I'm Ed Seay, these are my sons Chris, Robbie, and Brian, this is my father-in-law Bob Baldwin (Papa), and I have been the pastor of First Baptist Church Magnolia for 15 years now. I have five children and 12 grandchildren.

ROBBIE: I'm Robbie...Robbie Seay; I'm the worship pastor at Ecclesia. I'm a songwriter, father, husband.

 BRIAN: I'm Brian. I am the father of four; I am officially self-employed—I work for my brother-in-law on my wife's side, who is a musician. I do booking; we co-own a booking agency. I also teach a young adult Bible study called IKON (with a *K*) in Franklin, Tennessee.

 CHRIS: And you also make copiers...

 BRIAN: Oh yeah, and we make copiers. It's kind of like Paul's tentmaking; we sell copiers and then teach a Bible study. I was in Family Bookstore the other day, and I thought, it's pretty cool—my kids can go and see one uncle in the music section and go over to the book section and see another uncle. And I suppose if they went into the office of the bookstore, they could find one of my copiers. So we're all famous.

 CHRIS: And before that, Brian was a church planter—he planted a church in Austin. God moved him into copiers, I guess. *(Some laughter.)*

 PAPA: I'm Bob Baldwin, I've been married for 100 and— uh, 51 years, and I have five children, 12 grandchildren and 12 great-grandchildren. I pastored Mangum Oaks for 30 years, and then I retired—moved to the country where nobody could see me or hear me, then moved back so people could see me and hear me.

 DON MILLER: And Ed married your daughter...

 PAPA: And that was not supposed to happen...

DON MILLER: And that wasn't supposed to happen—are you still bitter about that?

 PAPA: Yes!

 CHRIS: Well, he built you a house—that's bound to heal some old wounds. *(Speaking to the reader)* Dad helped him buy this house, out of pure and complete guilt. But that is another story. Anyway, I am hoping this conversation will be sort of a transcript, like a PBS thing. I hope this book helps people to feel like a part of this family. I think it might give a rare window into the life of not only our family but of the church over the past 50 years. So I think that where we can be candid and passionate and loving and all those things combined, it might paint a really good and hopeful picture for the future of the church. So we will probably break for lunch; but until then, we will get as much on tape as we can.

 BRIAN: Can we eat Mexican food?

 DAD: We have a great Mexican restaurant.

 BRIAN: We don't have that in Tennessee.

 CHRIS: I figured there would be good Mexican food in Magnolia...

 BRIAN: It's not Pappasitos or anything...

 CHRIS: Pop, if we could start with you for a little bit, and the others can interject as we get going. Looking back on the years of ministry, you didn't make it rich, you spent a lot of years of service for a lot of people who moved on and did their own thing. Some you hear from regularly, some love you like a father, and others you probably don't hear from. When you look back now on leaving what you were doing and coming to the ministry, what do you feel? Where do you feel pride, and where do you feel regret?

 PAPA: Well, I don't think I have any regret for doing what I was doing in the ministry for all those years. Back in 1949, I began to feel the call to the ministry. I ran from it for a couple of years because that was the last thing I wanted to do. But finally, in April 1951, I answered the call to the ministry at Golf Drive Baptist Church in Houston. The pastor talked to me about it, and he told me that if you can do anything else, don't preach. Over the years, that's been one of the things I've told young men who have come to me: if you can do anything else—if you can be a plumber, a carpenter, if you can do anything—then God hasn't called you to preach. But as for me, I found that I couldn't do anything but preach. I preached two weeks after that, on a Wednesday night; I told them I didn't know what I would say, I didn't know how to preach, I didn't know if I could keep them long enough—and they told me that I did cause I preached for almost an hour and 50 minutes. Now, I don't know what I said, and they never did tell me what I said, and that just led on from there.

 CHRIS: You don't remember what the text was that you preached on?

 PAPA: Yeah, I think it was Colossians 2.

 DAD: That was right after the King James Version just came out.

PAPA: Well, it had been on the market about two years. But, whatever, I never regret that I started preaching. I worked at all kinds of jobs before I started to preach. I worked for Weingarten's, which was a chain store in Houston years ago; I worked at Hostess Cakes. I pastored my first church while I worked for Hostess. I tried to find things I could do and still have time to preach, too. My first church was China Grove Baptist Church, where I spent a few years.

 CHRIS: So working for Hostess is a respectable way of saying you drove the Twinkie truck, right? Did you get to drive that around to church and other places?

 PAPA: No, they wouldn't let me do that with the work truck. As far as me getting into the ministry, that's it. I never regretted the fact that I did. I had some ups and downs—I may get into that more later—but I think there are more ups than there are downs.

 CHRIS: Did you ever imagine that? I mean, part of the reason that we sit here is because you were faithful to that call; and, probably, if you hadn't been, then we wouldn't be in ministry and doing what we are doing. We all learned it from you; we are all pastors because you obeyed.

 PAPA: Well, I could never imagine that I would have a family with five children, three of them who are involved one way or another in ministry. All five of my children have been involved in the church, and so the grandchildren are involved in church. It's really an honor if I was a part of that. I think there are worse things that could happen to a family.

A LEGACY

We'll come back to the conversation in a minute. I just wanted you to get a flavor for what we're going to be doing from here on out. We'll be coming in and out of the dining room at Papa's house, as you and I will step outside every once in a while so I can explain some things and tell you how I'm feeling.

These are good guys all around. It's fun to have them here together. It's remarkable, really, to have a family of pastors and none of them, at least so far, have royally screwed up. I've always watched the other pastors in my life—pastors at nearby churches, friends I've met with similar vocations—just listening and learning. Everything did not come up roses for many of them. I watched as pastors left their families to pursue all the things they preached against. I've tried to stop many of them, warning them about sex and money and power. I've stared hypocrisy in the eyes more often than I can remember.

But in my own home, growing up under Dad, I saw the very best of a pastoring life. I was there in the hospital as we prayed for the sick, and I listened carefully to the counsel given to unnamed people who called our home in the midst of crisis. Love and patience seemed to embody the pastoral tone. I know this is true of most pastors, but I am grateful to be a part of a family where the position has been modeled well. I wonder if Papa or Dad ever stopped to think about the fact that they were modeling my future calling for me, that they were teaching me how to be a pastor, giving me a foundation.

When our lives are balanced and in order, love and patience abound. Some leaders in the church refer to me as a prophet—someone constantly challenging the church to change. I may have a prophetic edge, but when I am at my best, I am simply a pastor. And that means I care for people. I actually get in the mess of their lives, hold their hands, and walk them out of the wreckage. I am a teacher, storyteller, spiritual director, friend, mentor, and giver of hope. I am what my father was before me. I love it and I am made for it. Like Papa said, I *can't* do anything else. I just can't.

CHAPTER 2

SOME THINGS JUST CHANGE

How a Pastor Manages the Inevitable Shifts in Culture

This pastoral heart has never been more important than in the work I do with West End Baptist Church, where I lead a small congregation ranging in ages from 60 to 99. You heard me right: 60 to 99. So much for that 20-something postmodern label I seem to be stuck with. Every Sunday morning I pastor a congregation of people two to three times my age. Now to be fair, I also pastor a young congregation on Sunday evenings. But every Sunday morning for the last two years, I have put on a suit and tie and we sing a few hymns before we have our time of "special music," when someone (sometimes it's me) gets up to sing a beautiful and inspired bit of song, roaring straight out of the 1956 Baptist Hymnal.

And then I preach. I preach behind a gigantic pulpit fit for a politician. (I dare not venture down the steps. That would cause a scandal, to be sure.) I speak to this small, urban congregation of gray-haired men and women—men and women whose friends have recently passed, men and women who love to talk about their grandchildren and great-grandchildren, men and women whose bodies are beginning to deteriorate and whose memories are slowly fading—some of whom have spent a lifetime walking with Jesus. I love to sing to them (because they smile at me when I sing), but they often sleep while I preach—so I enjoy that less.

But my best moments with them are spent in hospices, hospitals, funeral homes, and at potluck suppers. They hurt and are often afraid and—despite the wisdom that comes with the years—unsure of what tomorrow will bring. I am humbled that these elderly, wise, and beautiful people are comforted by the hands and soft words of a 33-year-old man. Then I remember that it isn't just a man they believe they are talking to: it's their pastor. And the memories of Dad crying on the phone with a beloved member of the congregation, or of Papa praying half the night for one of his sick church members come back to me. Pastors don't give many answers—they just hold your hand, pray, shed tears, and join in the laughter at the right times. They remind people that they are not alone in the universe, that God is with them, and that God has sent a servant to be with them. It is strange to me, but to the members of our congregations, this companionship is more meaningful than a thousand right answers.

West End Baptist, the aging church I am talking about, has seen better days. After 30 years of steady decline in attendance from 1,000 to 40, a church will get desperate enough to merge with a radically missional emergent congregation. It makes sense—West End has what we need in terms of facilities and land, and we have people to fill the pews. But we are creatures of habit, and learning to encounter God in new ways is a lot like learning to walk all over again. It isn't easy. And so my West End congregation has had some difficulty merging with Ecclesia, who meets there on Sunday evenings.

When I stand in front of them, I feel like my grandfather because they look in many ways like his congregation. I want to honor them and their heritage as I honor my grandfather; the trick is that I must simultaneously attempt to lead them to a new place. The cards are stacked against us. The facilities are in disrepair. The location is ideal—central and visible—but it needs a complete overhaul. Convincing them to replace 60-year-old carpet is more arduous than running a marathon on one leg. They don't understand why we would want to replace all the carpet. It's perfectly good carpet and many of them helped install it only 50 short years ago. To be honest, there are times when I feel I am at my limit with this experiment—it has been exhausting from day one—and two years later, I feel it's getting harder each day, not easier. But I love these people and feel called to preserve their historic presence in our city. So what should I do? Why not ask the people you love the most? How do I love these people, how do I merge the old with the new? Let's go back into the dining room.

GENERATIONAL ISSUES: MUSIC AND TEACHING

 CHRIS: I love the people; I look at them and they look like the people I knew growing up. They dress the same way; they go to the same restaurants; they know the same places. In many ways they are the same, so I feel this connection with them and I know them. Some of my best moments with them are when they are in the hospital and they really need a pastor. But when it comes to leading them in the church, trying to affirm and honor their heritage, that's my biggest struggle. It's like we do in our family; we try to say, "We do church differently between the generations, and we honor and respect the different ways of doing it; but at the same time, we have to allow for that change." So I have to affirm them while at the same time I am bringing them to a new place.

 PAPA: You aren't going to bring them to where you want them.

 CHRIS: But I want to bring them to a place where they can reach out to more of the community, at least. They don't have to like the music we do on Sunday night, but can they do something that would be more appealing to the community they live in, at least?

 PAPA: I think at their age they just can't get out there. That's why they are where they are now—because they've lost that zeal of really trying to pull people into the church, and the younger generation is moving in around them.

 DAD: They are in the stage of life where they are not looking forward; they are looking backward. So whereas we are looking outward, they are looking inward. It's such a major paradigm shift.

CHRIS: It's more than they can do?

 DAD: And so like Pop said, they need a major population change among the body for anything to change.

 BRIAN: Part of the problem is that the people who are left are the ones who resisted the change to begin with. I look at First Baptist Church Amarillo, where I served, as an example of successfully bridging generations in the church. Now, they don't have the diversity of styles that Ecclesia and West End do; they had to meet somewhere in the middle. But they have hundreds of people from 60+ and hundreds of people that are 35 and below that are able to coexist in the same place. They still struggle with the problem of what that looks like on Sunday morning, what that is stylistically, how that translates into evangelism, and the different ways we do it. So maybe the prototype you struggle with is people who were resisting change when they were 25 or 30 and they have just remained the same.

 ROBBIE: Do you think the church has cycles just like we do, and maybe we are just here to hold their hands in the latter years of their lives? Maybe we lay this church down and move on with a new church, maybe in that same building, in that same community.

 CHRIS: Yeah, I mean, ultimately that has been the struggle for me. Now, I think that is good, and there's a place for that; but what they called me there to do was something different. It was to revive them, and instead I feel like the doctor trying to put them on life support for the last few years. I desperately want them to experience the joy of transforming the community together, in their lifetime.

DAD: But maybe now you need to get them off life support.

 CHRIS: Yeah, and the reality is that they don't really want to live that way. They don't want to, but they do. They want to be comfortable, and they want to be loved and be honored, but they think they want to step out and do something. I mean, that is what they say. But then again, some of the ones who were saying that the strongest when I got there were the ones who got sick and were in the hospital and passed away. So where there was a will to do something, it faded so quickly...

 PAPA: They want someone to preach to them and then let them go. They just don't want the church to die.

 CHRIS: That is what I respect so much: that they really do love that church and want that church to survive. But the question I constantly have to pose to them is, "Do we love this church more than we love the gospel?" You know, the gospel calls us to something bigger than just to have our church. It calls us to a kingdom mindset and a kingdom mentality. It says, can the kingdom move forward and can the cause of the gospel move forward? Hopefully those two can be synonymous...but maybe they're not.

 PAPA: That's not in their minds. They are at a point where that is no longer what they think about; they still just think about the traditional routines of Christianity.

 DAD: For them, letting Ecclesia share the facility is as kingdom-minded as they can be.

 CHRIS: For them that *is* being kingdom-minded; there are not many churches in their position. For example, this old deacon, probably their most dedicated deacon, was in his last days. The first time he came to the Ecclesia service, it was the first time he had seen the sanctuary full in 30 years. So he came up and hugged and kissed me and said, "What are you doing to make this happen?" And I told him, "We buy them beer." You know it's typically against Baptist beliefs to buy people beer to get them to come! And he said, "Well then, next week I'm buying." They want to see the church move forward; but the more [that friends of theirs] die, the more scared they get and things get harder. Maybe what I need to learn is just to love and pastor them. And that is what I have learned from you guys, from being in this family. That is what pastors do: we love them when they are scared, and we counsel them when things are hard. Instead, they don't understand that most people don't want to have [bars of] Dial soap on the side of the sink. Just making that change to soap dispensers was like we hurt somebody. It was like we did something wrong. The facilities look less than attractive, but just to change that [one small thing] was grueling. Everything we do like that sucks the life out of me, and at the same time I'm feeling like we need to be connected with some sense of history, and we as a church need to belong to them and vice versa.

 DAD: Remember when we were in Kings Bridge, and no matter what we did or how hard we worked that church wasn't going to grow because the nucleus we had were people nobody wanted to bond with. They were a group of dysfunctional alcoholics and addicts, and in a sense that's the problem you have there. No matter how good your preaching is and no matter how much you change the music, if they can't find that sense of community, which is what Ecclesia is all about...

 CHRIS: That is the hard part for me because these people have been together for a long time, and they really do know how to love each other. When somebody is sick or dies, and when we share meals together, they are fun. They are really funny and they enjoy each other. But you go preach to them, and they sit in a service and they fall asleep, and you'd think they don't like each other. But some of it is just the way they do church. Is that just the way churches were 30, 40 years ago, Pop?

 PAPA: Well, I think they have reached that age where friendliness is just not something they are overly zealous about. They are doing well just to be there on Sunday. Now at that age, you just aren't going to have that push to reach out to people, even to a minister who is there.

 CHRIS: I have a hard time preaching to them because on Sunday night people don't fall asleep—they actually listen to what I say. I mean, you can look at them and you can tell they are listening.

 BRIAN: Are we trying to decide if multigenerational churches are important? Can that still exist in this culture? Because more and more it doesn't. We have the seeker church creating this culture of families; and the emerging culture has created this focus on some young families, but mostly 20-somethings, college students, and progressive high school students. So we see less and less of multigenerational churches. I mean how important is that in the big picture?

 DAD: Somehow you have to connect generations because you have in Scripture the older women teaching the younger women, and Paul and Timothy. I mean, when you don't, you are violating one basic principle of discipleship.

 PAPA: But you have this in churches where they exist together, where the old is replaced by the younger. But at West End, you don't have that. That's why they are all up in age—you see that even if they move to Humble, they will still drive back for it.

 BRIAN: But the problem is that it doesn't just exist in the West Ends of the world; it exists in healthy postmodern emerging churches as well. You know 90 percent of them are 30 and under, and so the [idea of the] older teaching the younger is a 27-year-old teaching a 23-year-old.

 PAPA: In Magnolia, how many of the older group do you have, compared to the younger? I mean, they are sticking around. Now, I won't say all of them, but most of them want to stay in that traditional service.

 BRIAN: Have styles of music been the divisive factor that has moved us from multigenerational churches to not quite single-generational churches, but very close?

 DAD: I think it's a little broader than music, but I think that is the driving force. That's why we have to have two totally different styles, and when we try to blend the whole church, it doesn't work.

 CHRIS: And that's my biggest problem because I believe that churches are supposed to be multigenerational. I think we lose what you are talking about in Scripture—that the older ones teach the younger ones. In the same way, we have that dynamic in our family. People are always intrigued to ask, "Do your dad and grandfather learn from you guys?" So there are things that we do that you guys pick up on, and I would say yes, there are places in our conversations where we inform what you do and what you think and the transitions you guys make. And that dialogue is really important, but you get to that place where trying to make that happen in the church is so painful, and you just start to think, *I'm just going to give up on it.* That is where a lot of churches are. And I look in

the Scriptures, and I see in the book of Romans a defini-
tion of *maturity*. The people who are the most mature
are the people who bend for the immature. We are supposed to be flexible for the non-believers, and in reality
that is just not happening. I don't know anywhere that
is happening. Those who are supposed to be the most
mature—who have been in the faith the longest—are
the most inflexible. They are the ones who don't want
to bend. I just don't want to be that way as I get older.
I don't know; I may already be in that spot. But it's a
struggle to think, *If we are not going to be flexible, will
that ever happen?* I am not trying to put the blame on any
one generation, but if we are not flexible in styles and in
the ways we relate to each other—and they can't imagine doing discipleship any other way than Sunday school
in that neighborhood—then that isn't going to work. I
mean, nobody there wants to come sit in a classroom.

PAPA: We didn't have to worry about this because back
when I was doing it—I mean with evangelism—I just
had to preach a traditional evangelical sermon. Now they
want you to be a preacher-teacher; that didn't come to me
until I was just about to leave. But we had a group there
at Mangum Oaks who didn't want that. They wanted to
stay with that tradition. And when we went to the praise
and worship, they left—not many of them, but some of
them did. But some of the older group liked it; one of
them had even suggested it. But back then the evening
stuff was *it*. If you didn't have that evening service, you
didn't have church because somewhere in the Bible it
says that, and they swore to it, and now that is nearly
gone. Now Sunday school is slowly moving out, and it is
becoming weekday Bible studies. But to them, that was
not what the Bible says. It had to be on Sunday evening.

CHRIS: Where in the Bible is that, Pop?

PAPA: Robert's Rules of Order...

 CHRIS: Oh yeah, they added that to the canon, didn't they? I was wondering when they were going to do that. I didn't know it already happened...

 DAD: Talking about multigenerational churches—our church really is that. I think what allowed it to happen was that the people who had been there a long time allowed there to be change, as long as they could maintain a level of comfort. What they wouldn't allow is us forcing them to worship in a way that was foreign and uncomfortable to them. And even though it's not at their favorite time—they would prefer it at 11:00 a.m. rather than at 8:00 a.m.—as long as we gave them a worship service they could relate to, they were happy. What is neat is that when you get two generations outside of that worship setting, they interact, they work well together, they have so much in common—just don't get them started talking about worship.

 BRIAN: That's where I just laugh because, I mean, you look through Scripture and the thing that has divided us the most in the last 30 years of the church is not something that is prevalent in Scripture. It's not an important part of Scripture. Music is an important part of our culture, but when it comes to our faith, it is so secondary to everything else. But it is what has divided generations and split churches and what still defines us as a church. I mean, when you ask people about their church, you usually ask them about their preacher and about their music, and you're really asking about the style of music. But when you actually get people together doing something that is kingdom-minded—it may be community-based or service-based—something that's actually true worship, then we actually start to be a church. We keep trying to fit these generations into our music molds, and I think that is where we lose each other. Instead we need to say, "What can we do together outside of Sunday morning or Sunday night? What can we do in this community to actually impact those who live here?"

 DAD: For instance, we have people from both sides of the music divide. And then we do our big back-to-school project to give clothes and school supplies to needy kids, which is a major event we do. People are working side by side; there is no difference.

 BRIAN: Which is why you've been able to keep the generations.

 DAD: When we tried to do the blend—you know that fiasco—the people who liked praise and worship didn't make a big fuss; they just stopped coming. The traditional people were up in arms and ready to go to war.

 PAPA: I think it's not just the music. I think the preaching style has a lot to do with it, too, because when I left Mangum Oaks and we moved, I began to do expository preaching, and they didn't like that. They didn't want to learn; they just wanted somebody to go up there and preach to them for 30 minutes. They wanted the traditional old-time gospel message, not the teaching type of message.

 CHRIS: That's where what Brian is saying is common throughout the Bible. This has been the problem dividing the church from the beginning. It's culture, and it is just evidenced here in music. But that was the problem between the Jews and the Gentiles—it was a cultural divide, as in, "Our culture knows better than your culture." And when you have different cultures, those are the things that play out: what do you eat; what is your cultural voice in art, in music; how do you relate to each other. Because in reality, if you sit down to eat together or serve together, all those divides fade away pretty quickly.

 BRIAN: But even so, I disagree about the culture divide between generations. It is a big jump from there to the differences between a Jew and a Gentile, where the difference is life—the way you live, the way you eat, everything about your being. But we are all following the same God, and we can't take that away just because we have created these subcultures that become giants we can't get rid of. It's not equivalent.

 CHRIS: It's not completely equivalent, but the reality is that most of the Ecclesia people are radically different in their views about life and faith and politics and family. It's almost like they are the complete opposite of the 80- and 90-year-old people in the morning [service]. You know, the things like the Advent card we gave out at Ecclesia—it's beautiful, it has a picture of a woman in our church with her pregnant belly, and it talks about Advent as the time of waiting for the birth of Christ. We got rave reviews from Ecclesia, but a few of the folks at West End found it to be the most offensive thing they had ever seen—to show a woman's pregnant belly. That is so offensive to them. They think it's evil that I would ever let anybody show a woman's pregnant belly.

 PAPA: But 15 years ago, I wouldn't have ever thought of doing anything like that. It's just like they wouldn't allow someone with shorts to come in and sit in the front row. Somehow we've got to find a way to blend it, but I don't think you're going to find it because these older ones are so used to their traditional way of worship, and they are not going to get away from it.

CHRIS: I'm not sure I find a lot of hope in this conversation, but at least there's some sense that what we are trying to do is right. We need to try to do that, but it's not going to be easy.

 DAD: I find that in our church the people in the eight o'clock service are very pleased with it, and they wish we had the facilities to have it at eleven o'clock for them. But in venues other than worship, they love blending. In our 40 days of purpose and 40 days of community, in the home groups, and in the mission projects they absolutely love blending. They just don't want the music. I think every church has to find its niche as to what part of the culture they can be available to reach.

DIVINE MELODIES

As you can hear in our conversations, everything seems to come back to the practice of worship. Every generation hears a different voice when God speaks. In different phases of life God has sounded to me like George Burns, Darth Vader (a.k.a James Earl Jones), and Bono–I think my parents hear God's voice as a blend of Billy Graham and George Beverly Shea. There are some voices that are not God's voice at all, however. If you hear the voice of Pee Wee Herman or Michael Jackson it is safe for me to say you are not really a Christian. This might be a good time to put the book down and consider your eternal security.

In the same way God speaks to us in radically different musical styles–though we appreciate all kinds of good music my parents think Radiohead sounds like noise, while I hear beautifully intertwined melodies that lead me down a distinct and serene audible path. We are different, they see Branson Missouri as the epicenter of great music–to me it sounds more like the seventh circle of hell with golden bathroom fixtures. Our different tastes do not have to divide us, but the church has struggled to figure out how to celebrate this kind of diversity.

Music is not about entertainment for my generation. It is an art form we experience, it reveals the nature of the Creator. For these reasons music is incredibly personal. How do we nurture authentic worship and artistic value in a rapidly changing media saturated culture? We are one body, we drink from one cup, and share a common baptism—so why get so worked up about whether we use organs, guitars, or two turntables and a microphone?

 ROBBIE: What was it like to do ministry in the 50s, 60s, 70s...?

 PAPA: There has been a lot of change. I think things changed rapidly in the mode of worship, and in preaching. I don't know... Expositional preaching became a thing for the future, instead of just read a verse and go up there and blabber on. And I think you had to have a study, you had to have some way to outline what that verse meant; then I think the move from standard worship to praise and worship, was a big part of it.

 ROBBIE: At what point did that really start...in the 70s?

 PAPA: Um...seventy.....

 DAD: Early 80s, huh Pop? I was at San Jacinto 1979-80 and that was when it was really beginning to...

 PAPA: Maybe it was because Robert our son was the praise and worship leader, and I don't think there is a better one than he is...and he is the one that started it here. And the thing about it is that it wasn't started by the young people, it was started by older people. Some of the older people who had been somewhere that they heard it at and they said, "Well, let's try it."

 CHRIS: What do you think they liked about it?

 PAPA: I think it was the emotion; it stirred them up a little bit, those that could be stirred up. I think that was a tremendous change, in fact it still is. Like the church I pastored for a while in the country, you don't even talk about choruses, you either sing from the book or you don't sing.

 CHRIS: And you think the emotion made them uncomfortable?

 PAPA: I think the spirit made them uncomfortable.

 CHRIS: So as long as faith stayed a thing in their head, it was safe, but as soon as it became a thing of the heart....

 DAD: Don't you think during the 70s it was the whole Gaither gospel thing, when they were really big?

 PAPA: I think they led into the entire switch to praise and worship. Our choir did...what's that musical?

 DAD: *Hallelujah.*

 PAPA: Yeah, and the people just grabbed that. We did that twice; first in the auditorium, then we came back and announced that we were going to do it in the gym and we had the gym packed out, of course the acoustics weren't that great.

DAD: Yeah, it really wasn't in the praise and worship vein, but it was the emotion and the heart that transitioned into that...because before then worship was tradition, you just sang the hymns...

PAPA: Whatever was in the bulletin, that's what we did, you didn't move away from that. You got in the auditorium, you had prayer, a song, announcements, two more songs, you did special music and then the preacher.

BRIAN: So it led worship services to be more spontaneous.

CHRIS: Which is interesting, because when we talk about the postmodern influence...that is really the beginning of that in a lot of ways. What they were saying was, "I don't really want to know what you know, I want to experience something bigger than me"...that's the hunger that was created at that point.

PAPA: And if you varied any from what they see printed, they wanted to know why..."The bulletin doesn't say we do that now, why are we doing that now?"

DAD: And there was comfort in that structure and tradition.

CHRIS: Control...you could control it....

ROBBIE: Do you think you had to change what you did from say 1955 to 1995...?

PAPA: I fought against it, but I felt like I had to.

 BRIAN: Did you change how you preached?

 PAPA: I just went up there and preached an old hard evangelistic sermon... I said "You're lost and going to hell if you don't get saved..." And I realized I had to preach a more expositional type message, I had to actually learn them something, they had it where I could teach and they could learn.

 CHRIS: Now as that is changing, because some of the transition now is even when we are teaching, in some contexts like in Dad's more, the pastor is still seen as an authority so you can get up and teach and instruct and people accept some of what you say as coming from an authoritative source. In our context not so much anymore; so what I have to do now ask more questions...I have to ask really good questions. I talk about us returning to this Hebrew Midrash style of learning, instead of this didactic style of teaching, where these are the things you need to know. I have to spend more time asking the right questions. That's a lot of changes in the last 40 or 50 years in the way we do things...that's at least three and probably more totally different preaching styles. There is very little in common from the evangelistic hellfire and brimstone to the teaching-oriented exegetical preaching style and very little from that to this more Midrash oriented narrative preaching style.

 DAD: And there is no one right approach, you have to hit people at the point of their need, you have to hit them in a way that they will be open, to try to force one style on another group if they're not open to it...

BRIAN: But there are a lot of preachers ignoring what their group really needs...

 ROBBIE: That's what I want to hear; did you think through the years having to adjust with the way the times went?

 PAPA: I felt like I had to, but for a long time I didn't...I wasn't going to be pushed into this and really the only reason I didn't want to be pushed is because I didn't know what I was doing. I had to spend a long time thinking about what it meant for me to do this.

BRIDGING THE GAP

I have no idea how we'll accomplish the goal set before us to merge West End Baptist and Ecclesia. On paper, no two congregations have been more different; but we belong to the same body and we are better together than we are separated. Right now, I pastor two different churches and try to serve as a guide through the pains of compromise for the good of the whole church.

For Baptists, particularly in Texas, the 1950s were a little taste of what heaven must be like. No doubt about it—these were the good old days. Baptismal waters were stirring, church softball leagues were hitting, and these royal ambassadors for Christ were at the top of the cultural heap. Faith was so much simpler before the hippie sexual revolution and the postmodern invasion. Once you'd been dunked, all you needed was the Bible, the Baptist hymnal, and a good Sunday school class. Here's to days gone by!

To evangelical and mainline churches struggling to find their rhythm again, the challenges of the 21st century seem like a bad episode of *The Twilight Zone*. May the church come together and move into the future together. Ecclesia and West

End hope to forge a path for dying urban churches and young fledgling emergent churches. Here's to the past—not just for the sake of the past, but also for how it leads to our future.

I learn a great deal from my fathers. I have learned I am not the only one who has had to transition a church. I have learned that either transition happens or churches die—it *must* happen—and that a pastor must navigate the changes or lose his congregation completely. But I have also learned that change must be gentle, that everything must be done in love. And if I come across people who do not want to change, I go back to my other calling: I hold their hands.

CHAPTER 3

THE INNER LIFE

How a Pastor Keeps his Sanity in an Insane World

We don't remember what happened in those former times. And in future generations, no one will remember what we are doing now. Ecclesiastes 1:11

Happiness is not my goal; I don't want to spend my life making decisions based on what I *think* I want. But I know a lot of miserable people (read: pastors), and I do not want to join their lot. I am blessed with a loving family, a beautiful home, a hospitable climate (for nine months of the year), and boundless opportunities. Yet I am fully aware that I could fall into the pit at any time.

I was recently in the home of Lyman Coleman, the founder of Serendipity, who at age 72 offers a lot of insight to a young man like me. He is an accomplished man who has exhibited enormous positive influence on the church. One could call him the "Father of the Small Group Bible Study Movement." But in the midst of a hectic life spent writing books, creating Bible study materials, and speaking at conferences, he fell into a hole he couldn't crawl out of. So he cancelled everything on his calendar and stayed in his basement for over two years. Isolated. Depressed. Alone.

Lyman's wife picked up the pieces of their life, paid the bills, cared for the children, and prayed for her husband. She met Lyman while she was working as Billy Graham's assistant, and they fell deeply in love—that love and her faith sustained her during those dark days. Lyman was questioning everything; he didn't have any answers, but the questions kept coming. He began to write them down, pore over the Scriptures, and write more questions. The ensuing struggle with the Scriptures became the light at the end of this dark tunnel. The poetry of the Psalms, the parables of the Messiah, and the apostles' letters were a balm to his wounds. Life and hope began to return, and this list of questions eventually became the *Serendipity Study Bible*, the Bible I used to lead countless Bible studies in high school and college.

I know for a fact that hardship and difficult times give birth to beautiful movements of God. At times, this will be the pastor's lot. It is unfortunate; however, God is in it, and when we are finished, we will love him all the more for putting us through the trials. There are some weeks when I feel I'm just two really bad events away from crawling into my basement and withdrawing from the rest of the world. My life is good, but it is unmistakably fragile. I don't want to see it fall apart. So when we started talking to my grandfather about his darkest days in ministry, I was determined to listen and learn.

DEPRESSION

 CHRIS: Do you think you were ever depressed?

 PAPA: Yes, the last three years of my pastorate at Mangum Oaks—yeah, real depressed! There were times I didn't even go to the office; I just went there Sunday, preached, and that was about it. But it ended, and it was over with, and we had a good send-off, I thought. When we retired, they gave us a good retirement party. We had a couple of people who tore the church up even after we left, and the church is dead because of that. And wherever they go—I don't know if they are still in church or not—but wherever they go the same thing will happen.

 CHRIS: So what does that feel like? I mean, that's your life's work, and it wasn't invested in the building or the institution—what you were really investing in was the people, and you look at that with great pride. But when you see people destroy what you spent your life working on, it must sting.

 PAPA: It hurts. It hurts to look back on it and see that there were some who held on, who continued to do a fairly good job—still in church, still working in the church. And there were a few who were just playing church, and I did that the last few years in Mangum Oaks Baptist Church—I spent time playing church, that's all.

DAD: As you look back on those tough years, what do you think you could have done differently or what could someone have done for you? That's got to be a peril of a long pastorate, and I've only been in Magnolia half as long as you were there.

 PAPA: Well, I can't say it was the long pastorate that did it, even though I look back on it and think it could have been. But I never had any real difficulties because one of the things I prayed was, *Lord, don't let me stay here too long. Let me know when it's time to go.* And I think he really did that when I retired because he said, "That's enough." And I left. I don't know. As I look back on it, I have tried to say what I could have done differently. Probably one of the things is don't give up, or when you want to give up, get out of there. But I didn't. I just gave up...I had burnout.

 DAD: I guess my question is what could someone have done to keep you from getting down in that hole and wanting to give up? I look back on that ministry where we relocated the church when Inwood Forest was new and booming and growing, and then it finally got to the point where with the economy and all it began to decline, and the church always mirrors the community it's in. And that became a tough time for any church. What could you or someone else have done to keep it from becoming a depressing situation? Or was there anything that could have been done?

 PAPA: I don't know. I talked with the Union Baptist Association; I talked with some of the people at Baptist General Convention of Texas. I had some of them down at the church for a week. They went through the church, the roll, the neighborhood around us; not many of them had an answer. The only answer I know would have been to keep me from becoming depressed, as I did. Trying to reach down and grab my bootstraps and pull myself out of there. But I don't know that I really wanted to...

 DAD: Do you think a sabbatical would have helped?

 PAPA: I think so—in fact, I thought about that. I never took one.

 CHRIS: You had been there almost 30 years and never had a sabbatical?

 PAPA: No, in fact I was doing well just to get a vacation.

 DAD: Well, that takes out a lot of mystery about the burn-out right there.

 CHRIS: Yeah, I mean, if you had been given time regularly to just go and read, study, pray...

 PAPA: I think so, yeah. I should have done that. Pastors need to do that.

 DAD: Just to be exposed to an encouraging situation...

 CHRIS: Yeah, but one of the best things going was that you had pastor friends, right? Did that help?

 PAPA: Yeah, and I met with them; there were about five or six of us. We would get together a great deal and pray and talk about each other's churches and make suggestions about what we could and couldn't do.

 CHRIS: People who deeply love you, and you love them still to this day.

PAPA: I guess they do; some of them are gone. In fact, there's only one left.

 CHRIS: And he's right down the road from me.

 PAPA: He's 80-something years old.

 BRIAN: So they were older pastors...

 PAPA: Yeah...older than me. That was a good thing. That prolonged my time there, just being with people I could talk to who were sharing the same problems. Very important.

Papa went on to talk about depression, about burnout, about his wanting to give up. I have been there, too, and not just when things were going bad. At age 23, the church I started had exploded into a large and influential ministry; the circumstances of life were good. But I lived on the verge of tears, which was not a bad thing. I was dependent on God in a way I had never been before. The danger is when that fragility turns to sorrow, bitterness, and depression or sinful escapes. As a young single pastor, I lived with a sense of vulnerability that was inescapable.

Depression in ministry is the beginning of bad things, not the end of them. Without a sabbatical, without time alone or with family or with God, doors get opened that shouldn't be opened. I know that a lot of depression is relational: relationships with ourselves, with our friends, with our spouses, and with God. So when depression comes, it is usually because some relational thing is out of whack. This sets us up for all kinds of trouble.

FEMALE ADVANCES

Every pastor is a kind of sex symbol. Put a man in a suit, stand him before a congregation and let him speak with authority—and girls are going to want to latch on to him, looking for the love of an important man, looking for security. I asked Papa about this:

 CHRIS: So if you didn't have those friends, you probably would have fallen into depression a whole lot earlier, and if you had been in depression when these women were coming and declaring their undying love for you...

 PAPA: I probably would have fallen into it. I look back—and in fact Betty and I have talked about it—because when anything like that happened (women making advances), she always knew it; in fact, she made many a trip—either her, or Sharon, or Lisa—to the office for these so-called counseling sessions with these ladies. She would sit down in the office, and we would leave the door open. She spent many nights sitting there waiting for me to get finished counseling this gal. One of our deacons finally fell into it; one of the ladies who had come after me then pursued him, and he fell for it.

 CHRIS: Well, when you watched that happen, at least you had some sense of *that could have been me.*

 PAPA: Well, the deacon's wife kept saying to me, "Brother Bob, that could have been you—she was after you too." And I know...it could have been me.

 DAD: Think of the repercussions that could have had through the generations. It would have affected all of us. It's not likely we would be serving God the way we are today, and we would not be in this room talking about it.

PAPA: I had a pianist that followed me, and that could have had some big repercussions, too—she was part of Grace Memorial and Mangum Oaks, and it was very difficult to have her there. That could have gone bad.

 CHRIS: Now we realize the same kind of thing could happen to us.

PASTOR FRIENDS

I don't remember my grandfather being the most handsome man on the block. The pictures of Noni indicate that she was quite a looker in her day, but Papa seemed to be a bald, middle-aged chick magnet. Unexplainable? No, his passion for Christ and natural charisma garnered attention. I thank God for his devotion to family and cannot ignore his warning that if these women had been pursuing him while he was depressed and spiritually lifeless, things might have turned out differently.

I've been thinking a great deal about this inner life—the life of depression and false medication—wondering how to protect myself from this sort of thing. I drove 80 miles this morning just to walk on the beach and pray—it seemed like an extravagant self-indulgence. But the truth is, keeping my heart and mind clear, stopping to pray, turning off the blasted cell phone— these may be the most important gifts I can give to my family, to myself, and to my congregation. In the end, it's days like this that may keep me healthy, well, and together.

You could see my grandfather's eyes light up while he talked about his pastor pals and anything else that brought real impact on people's lives. Being a pastor is what he loves. And there is no question this was the calling on his life and that his life bears the fruit of obedience—not only in his life, but also in countless other lives.

Why don't I have pastor friends like my grandfather had—men who meet regularly for coffee, laughter, friendship, and support?

    1) One of the negative results of the church growth movement is an increased focus on comparison, which gives birth to a sense of competition. Too often, I sit with a group of pastors whom I genuinely like, and I know we could be friends and would all be better off, but the room is tainted with the stench of fragile egos busy performing for one another.

    2) The post-Christian culture has created such diversity among churches (ethnic, language, Boomer, contemporary, emergent, postmodern, mega) that some of my peers live in a completely different world. Though we may be the same age and share many things in common, the immediate fruits of time spent together are not easily harvested.

TAKE CARE OF YOURSELF

To love hurting people is exhausting, and I could not ignore the way Papa's gaze saddened when we talked about his three years of depression. We are frail human beings. Working for God does not make us invincible—it only makes our failures more painful.

When we find ourselves in that situation, we can find ways to care for ourselves. Schedule a retreat. Go see a movie, or just sit on the beach somewhere and gaze into a shell. A decision to slip into sin will not only kill us, but it will also kill our children, their children, and so on. I know it's a hard life, but it's also a rewarding life. Every life comes with some struggle. What we do with that struggle may bring the bounty of decades of harvested fruit or acres of rotten crops. Get some time alone, and then you also need to surround yourself with pastor friends who are not competing with you, but are speaking encouragement in your life.

CHAPTER 4

FAMILY

How a Pastor Keeps his Family Together

My brother Brian tells stories about a guy back in Amarillo, Texas—a guy who used to ride his bike all over town, and every time you saw him he'd be wearing a different hat. One day it would be a hard hat, the next a fishing cap, and another time a bright orange construction hat with a figurine from a trophy glued to the bill. His name was Mr. Luke, and everybody in town knew about him and liked him. It's an old cliché that we have to wear different hats throughout life—some of them feel natural and some are a bit absurd. The cliché of different hats is especially true of pastors. There are times when I walk into a room and feel as though I'm wearing a bright orange cap with a figurine glued to the bill. But in the end, I know these people need a pastor—right here, right now—so I wear the hat. Pastors have to be so many different people in so many different situations. We've all done funerals the same weekend we've done weddings.

When I hear stories about pastors' families, the realization sets in that I do not wear my hats of father and husband quite as well as I wear the ones involved in the calling of a pastor. The simultaneous call of being a husband, father, son, brother, friend, and pastor is often too overwhelming for a person to do all of them well. There always seems to be someone peering in the window of my glass house to watch me sipping coffee and cursing at the Astros' box score. The pressure of being a parent and a spouse is heavy enough without the church peering in, waiting for you to mess up.

Now that I know what it's like to be a pastor and a father, I regret some of the trouble I caused my dad when I was a kid. I wish I'd understood how difficult he had it. And while I always loved my dad, I could have walked up to him a few more times, looked him in the eye, and said, "I respect you. You are a great man." Too often I was silent when he probably needed me to speak. But it wasn't easy for me, either. The expectations of being a pastor's child often led to rebellion, spiritual cynicism, and a relational divide between parent and child.

MINISTRY, KIDS, AND A WIFE: THE BALANCING ACT

As we came back to the table, I wanted to talk about family, about raising kids—the most important hat God has given us to wear. Personally, this was an important conversation for us to have, regardless of the book. I realized that our five lives accounted for 19 children, 23 grandchildren, and 12 great-grandchildren, all ranging in age from 50 to one still forming in his mother's womb.

 CHRIS: Where do we start here?

 DON MILLER: How do you keep a family together?

 PAPA: You love them, no matter what they do. You love your wife.

 CHRIS: How do you keep your wife on your team for so long?

 PAPA: You love her; love her more today than you did yesterday. I can't emphasize this enough. You love your wife. Figure out how, if you have to, but that is what you have to do. That is what her heart wants, and she deserves it.

 BRIAN: Did you ever feel like the church wanted more of you than you could give? Or did you look back on a period of years and realize, you know, *I was married to the church* for that time frame?

 PAPA: You know what I did when I realized I wasn't spending time—not necessarily with the family, but with my wife—as much as I should? I would do a series about the family, and I would talk about the husband and wife. And every three months—even more than that—I would take my wife away for the weekend, go somewhere by ourselves, leave on a Friday and get back on Sunday morning. It goes back to taking time, you know. Believing the primary call on your life is to your family and the secondary call is to your congregation. Both are very important, but one is more important than the other.

 BRIAN: I'm not a workaholic, and so my issues tend to rise up not from working too much. But I think it's what you just said. I think I do a good job with my children, but after work—by the time I play with my kids—I wonder how much energy I have left to really tend to Amy's needs? I wonder how you guard against that, with having a lot of kids? How do you have any energy left to be a husband after you've been a pastor and a father most of the day?

 CHRIS: They're both completely emotionally taxing. People want a lot from you, and kids *demand* a lot from you.

 PAPA: Well, that could be like my son. Terry carried a little red wagon next door to the neighbor one time and said, "Mr. Vernon, could you fix this wagon for me?" And he said, "No, I can't do that, let your daddy fix it. He wants to do that." And Terry said, "Oh, my daddy ain't got time to do that—he's a preacher." He said it just like that, and that was when he was six years old. I've seen a lot of preachers whose kids feel the same way; they haven't got any time for them. And I've seen a lot of preachers' families who are in trouble because they didn't spend much time together, and that is one of the things I always preached: God, family, and church, but church always has to fall in there behind the family.

 CHRIS: And you think that's part of why you have a family that is continuing in the ministry?

PAPA: I don't know if that's all of it, but I think it has a lot to do with it. I wanted them there at church. I didn't make my kids go, but they knew I wanted them there. And I started taking some days off to spend with the family. It was important for the kids to know they were more important than my church. I began to make changes there, to spend time with my wife, rather than go up to the church. I didn't do it that often, but when I really did take a day off, it was for the family. We used to let the kids decide where they wanted to eat. It was usually Friday night, and one good thing was that they always wanted to go to Doyle's (a favorite family restaurant to this day), but I think that's the most important thing you can do—love your wife more today than you did yesterday, and love your family the same.

 CHRIS: How did both of you deal with the expectations put on your kids just because they were *your* kids?

 PAPA: I think they knew that we lived in a glass house, especially at Mangum Oaks. We had some problems with that, where they were watched by the deacons' kids, and the way we got around that is we didn't let them play with the deacons' kids.

 DAD: I think it was that we weren't trying to live up to anybody's expectations. And I think my goal was to try not to cram all of my ideas down your throats, but to teach you to follow the Lord, to find God's plan and seek his will and his truth. And I thought that if you did that, then all the other stuff would just come.

 PAPA: I think you can look at the three of you and see he didn't raise you up right.

 ROBBIE: Pop, look at me, what's wrong with me...? *(Robbie is holding up his hands in mock protest)*

DAD: Other than a bad hair day?

 CHRIS: It's been a bad hair month.

 ROBBIE: Brian's had a bad 10 years—

 BRIAN: It's been a bad hair decade.

 CHRIS: Just to *have* a hair day would be good.

 DAD: You know I think there were times, like with this church here, where we went in saying, "Don't expect us to live up to any certain image or expectations; we are going to be who we are." And in this little mission church we jumped into in the late 80s, they had those expectations and we just rejected them. I mean, they were psycho people, and we just weren't going to fall into that.

 PAPA: We went into that saying, "Betty doesn't play the piano, and I'm the pastor and she isn't. So if you want her to play the piano, she won't; and if you want her to be the pastor, she doesn't want to."

 CHRIS: But Noni's Sunday school class was one of the best Sunday school classes in the church.

 PAPA: You should have heard some of the phone calls we got from people saying how much they love us, but especially her—because of what she taught them in Sunday school. You know, she told them, "If your husband runs around on you, don't divorce him, just get a gun and shoot him." One night we got a telephone call and this woman had the gun out, her husband's clothes were burning out in the backyard, and she was waiting for him to get home. We said, "No, no, wait—don't shoot him!" And she said, "You told us to!" So Noni had to get on the phone and talk her out of it.

 BRIAN: I guess my biggest fear right now is not that I'm going to screw up with my kids, but that I'm going to screw up with my wife. That I'm going to be a good father and I'm going to be a good minister—or whatever my job is—but in the end I won't have the energy to be a good husband and be there for my wife. As a pastor and a father, especially in those times with little children when the energy levels just aren't there, how do you keep on feeding the relationship what it needs?

 DAD: Well, I think it's about boundaries and priorities. With the church you've got to have boundaries so that it doesn't take more of you than you are able to give, so you still have enough to give your family. As strange as it sounds, you've got to prioritize the relationship with your wife over your children, but that doesn't mean you exclude your children. If you don't give your relationship with your wife what is needed, it doesn't matter what you do with your kids—they won't have what they need. So you've got to make sure you invest in that relationship first.

 PAPA: They've got to see that you love her.

 CHRIS: Probably all of our kids would say that, and it's easy enough to just stay out of trouble, but it's going over and above when we are both tired and exhausted. We are both good with each other, but it's not what we wanted.

 DAD: But if all you have to give is times of exhaustion, then the issue is the boundaries.

CHRIS: Which is part of what Pop said. I think we're learning about finding time and re-tooling because life has been constant, and this isn't working.

 DAD: And maybe it's easier in retirement, but at least in full-time ministry, it's still a struggle for Mom and me. We have periodic times of very frank discussion on one end or the other, or both, when the boundaries have bled over into the time we have for each other and for Jess. But if you don't manage your life, then it will manage you; ministry will take every bit of you that you will give it.

 PAPA: A weekend together away...

 BRIAN: All my wife wants to do is sleep when we go away.

 PAPA: That's up to you. *(Papa chuckles)*

 DAD: Maybe sometimes it needs to be more than a few days, and the first couple of days may be physical recovery; but you know it's something that has to be managed.

LOVE AND AFFECTION: YESTERDAY AND TODAY

 PAPA: One of the things I look back on was the fact that I didn't help [my wife] with the kids as much as I should have. Maybe it's because I wasn't home. I'd get home at 11 o'clock at night and left at 7 o'clock in the morning. I could use that as an excuse, but I thank the Lord that I see you guys working with your wives, next to your wives, and doing some of the things that normally a lot of husbands would think are the wife's responsibility.

DAD: Don't you think that's a generational thing, though? I think my generation is more involved than yours, and that theirs is more involved than mine.

 CHRIS: There are a lot of people in our church who say, "I don't want to advance in my career." When they are offered a promotion, they don't take it because they know it means more time away from their kids. That was unheard of 20 or 30 years ago, to know you could make more money and not choose that.

 BRIAN: I wonder how much of that is the shift in marriage and divorce. When you grew up there might have been unhappy marriages in either your family or with people you knew, but divorce didn't happen because that was not acceptable. But for our generation, we grew up and saw divorce happen, and we would point at the reasons why divorce happened. Our generation looked at it and said, "My parents split up because my dad was never home, and he worked and cared about getting a promotion more than he cared about us," or whatever it was. So we're trying to compensate for those areas and change the way we parent and live. We will fail in some areas, and our kids will try to compensate for those areas, and so it's the cycle of parenting and living.

 DAD: I think it's that, and I think it's just the changing paradigm of the roles of husbands and wives, father and mother. I think 40 or 50 years ago the father was the breadwinner, he was the unquestioned authority, and he was to be served.

 CHRIS: So in proportion to that—I don't know if we are a perfect test for this—but you went from never saying "I love you" or showing physical affection, to showing it some, to showing it a little bit more. Now you watch us with our kids, and I almost begin to worry, *Wow, all we do*

is just hug them and kiss them and tell them we love them. I mean, the shift in that is amazing. Do you remember Ma-maw *(Papa's mother)* ever saying, "I love you" and hugging you?

 PAPA: Never once, and I don't know...because a man during that time just didn't say that. They didn't show that compassion, and a mother might try to show that, but she never would say it.

 DAD: And we still, in the redneck culture out here, see some of that. There are some who are a throwback to that old paradigm of family roles. But it isn't a better paradigm. Love is best. Showing it is.

 BRIAN: What about this: all of us kids have had times when we really screwed up. For instance, what about the time I stole a car and got drunk and I was in the seventh grade? I use that example a lot because of how you dealt with it. Because to me, as a parent now, that was full of wisdom and it was a great way to deal with it. Granted, it was six months later when you found out about it. But when you begin to have that troubled child, whether it's a short- or long-term issue, how do you deal with that as a pastor, in the public sphere as well as in the private sphere? There is a pastor out in a Houston suburb whose kids were into drugs, and it cost him his job. And it went into this spiral where now he has left his wife for this other woman. How do you deal with this idea of the spiral of the public and private spheres not being separate?

 DAD: Well, with you there never was a habitual pattern. Now, there was the occasional stupid act, which is just part of growing up. You just have to give some grace there and say, "Well, I did my share, but my kids are not bad kids; they are not punks, they're not drunks, they are not drug addicts; they are just kids growing up." And then you don't deal with it as a pastor; you deal with it as a father. The public sphere...I couldn't care less what they thought. That wasn't my concern—y'all were my concern. Now, if someone made it an issue, then I dealt with that; but it never got to the point where it was a threat to my ministry.

 CHRIS: Because even if we screwed up, we never had that label because Dad didn't allow that or treat us that way.

 DAD: And what if I had pulled you aside and said, "Do you have any idea what you could do to our church? Do you know what you could do to my image as a pastor?" If you deal with your kids with a focus on that, then you build resentment and your kids don't feel nurtured and loved and cared for—they feel used. I think it's all in how you frame it. We came to you and said, "Look, you messed up. The real issue is what the Lord wants you to do. Is your life focused towards pleasing the Lord? It's not about my image, my job, my feelings; it's about your relationship with the Lord." We tried to teach y'all how to pursue Christ, and I think that if pastors made that their focus with their kids, then they would not have nearly as many problems. I think that once you deal with it wrong, it begins to build walls between them and you, the church, and their faith.

 CHRIS: And part of that goes back to what I was asking. That is a much more intimate approach. And if you look at our child-raising styles, ours will probably be even more intimate than that. It really recognizes the relationship as the centerpiece. If you're not in the place where you can be loving and affectionate, then you can't really have that.

 DAD: Well, I'll tell you what it doesn't do; it doesn't raise kids that are just like you. People look at us and say,

"Wow, your kids have accepted your values and example." Well, you have the core...and obviously from some of our conversations there is a huge difference in the way we see things. But I think that is the weakness of a fundamentalist approach. They try to take all the rules and regulations and superficial things, and sooner or later kids see that as artificial and reject it.

 BRIAN: One might call that legislating morality. *(A jab at longstanding political debates in the family.)* I think the greatest compliment to how you handled us when we had problems is that you didn't make it about you. It was not about how it affected you, or what it did to your career. I remember that specific instance where I went out and got drunk, you said to me, "You want to try that, that's fine. Come and get me next time, and I'll take you to the liquor store, and I'll get you liquored up."

 CHRIS: Let's do it tonight, Dad! *(laughter)*

 BRIAN: But you let it be my issue, and you didn't place the pressure of what the church would think on a 12-year-old.

 DAD: I think a lot of pastors are under the impression that they have to keep their image. I think most churches are actually drawn to people who are authentic, even with faults and weaknesses.

 CHRIS: Which is exactly why we need to post that picture of Mom on the New Year's Eve of the millennium—then we could say we relate to you!

WHEN THEY MESS UP

There I was, sitting at the table, knowing my girls would be teenagers before I knew it, that my son would probably come home after having had a bit too much to drink, and I would have to deal with it. It comforted me that I wouldn't be the first pastor to have to deal with it. And it comforted me, too, to know that my church isn't as important as my wife or my kids. My wife needs to know she is the most important thing in my life. And my kids need to know that even though I am a pastor to many, I am a father to them.

My father and grandfather spoke with wisdom and confidence during this conversation. They weren't confused about how or why they did what they did. And we aren't a perfect family, but we don't resent them or dislike them, we respect and love them. I want my kids to be able to say that I loved them, and that they are lovable people, and that God loves them just as I love them. My father and my grandfather are able to look back and see the fruits of balancing family and ministry, as well as point out the pitfalls for those of us who have no real perspective.

In our relative fame, success, respect, or any other aspect of ministry, we need to remember that those closest to us are the first ones we minister to. Their needs come first, not our needs to be respected by our peers. Our wives need loving husbands, and our kids need to have loving fathers. In an effort to see ourselves as important and successful, we might be ignoring the fact that in our own homes there are "little red wagons" that need to be fixed and that it's not our neighbors' jobs to fix them. I am especially thankful for this conversation. The lessons were simple, but they may have a greater impact on more people than any other conversation we engaged in previously.

CHAPTER 5

A STUDY IN POWER

How a Pastor Navigates Theological Differences

The gospel is about reconciliation between God and humankind, as well as between people. So when the gospel is used to divide, which Paul often speaks against, it becomes unChristian, and, for that matter, unbiblical. This is the current state of Christianity—we are divided by our views of God, Scripture, church polity, baptism, culture, the Apocalypse, gender, sexuality, morality, and the like. I have heard it said that the Reformation is the best and worst thing that ever happened to the church.

I, for one, have had enough. Theological conversations are a privilege granted to those who have encountered a living God. But many have chosen the pursuit of knowledge about the Divine as a substitute for a divine relationship. In other words, rather than humbling themselves before God to receive unconditional affirmation, they seek it through their own smarts. It's rather silly. The Scriptures are intended to point us toward the Creator, not enable us to understand everything about the Creator and his ways. Early attempts at theological discourse were about bringing us together around the essence of the gospel. It's time to return to the basics while embracing all believers and the reality that our knowledge is very limited. Let's start with the apostles' attempts to articulate the gospel.

THE ESSENTIALS OF THE FAITH

 CHRIS: The Apostles' Creed...

 PAPA: Did they write a creed?

 CHRIS: Apparently they did. But seriously, this was an attempt to wrap up the essence of God the Father-Creator, the Son, the Virgin Mary, the reality that Christ died, that he descended into hell, rose on the third day, and ascended to heaven where he is at the right hand of God, where he judges the living and the dead. Our belief in the Holy Spirit, the church, communion of saints, forgiveness of sins, resurrection of the body, and life everlasting. And we've spent our lives seeing where denominations have been adding to the essentials of faith, adding certain statements about the Bible. They have said, "If you don't believe this, then you aren't in—or at least you're not in with us." Is that a proper summary of what is actually essential, or is there more to it?

 DAD: Well, I don't know if I would agree with your assessment of what Southern Baptists have done. We have always said we are not a creedal people.

 CHRIS: I'm not just talking about Southern Baptists—in fact, I have not mentioned Baptists at all. But it is interesting that you assume that; a lot of denominations have picked one thing or another and are devouring one another about secondary theological issues.

 DAD: So are you saying that we have wasted time on unnecessary expansion?

 CHRIS: Yeah, and how important are those things? Are they worth getting divided over, and are they worth spending time on?

 PAPA: Are we getting divided over those things?

 CHRIS: I guess we could say that we are more divided over power and lust for power. I think people use theological issues to say, "Will you submit to me and my agenda or not?"

BRIAN: The nature of Scripture—that was the biggest theological debate of your ministry time. That is a little bit different. I mean, the Apostles' Creed doesn't deal with inerrancy, mainly because they didn't have a canon. Do you think we spend too much time on that? Is the inerrancy of Scripture essential to someone's salvation experience?

DAD: I don't think that it is essential to someone's salvation, but it is essential to sound doctrine. You can be saved and not have sound theology related to Scripture, but you cannot form solid theology and practice without sound theology of Scripture.

CHRIS: But don't you think that some of that debate is really about semantics? One person is saying it's authoritative, the other says it is without error. Dad says it's without error of any kind, and we don't even have the original manuscripts, so it's a hypothetical discussion. Because the reality is that we read the same story in two different books, where a certain number of people were mentioned here and it was a different number of people there. Is that an error? Well, the point isn't really the number of people that were there.

DAD: I really don't want to get into that kind of debate. I believe that Scripture is authoritative, and I believe it is without error. I think it is the standard by which we build faith and practice and theology. I do think we have spent far too much time on things that are not at the core of that debate.

PAPA: I think what we are seeing in these arguments now is that this group just wants more power. Before I even retired, I stopped going to conventions because what they were doing at these conventions didn't make any sense. It was just that this one wanted more power than the other one. The theological differences they were arguing made no sense.

 CHRIS: So Dad, if you say the Bible is without error of any kind, and I say that the Bible is perfect in every way it needs to be perfect—how different are those statements, in your estimation?

 DAD: My only problem with that is who decides in what areas it needs to be perfect? If you say Scripture has errors, then someone has to decide what those errors are, and I just see that as a dangerous and inappropriate approach. We may disagree about that, but if you put yourself as the judge of Scripture, then I think that is a dangerous paradigm.

 Chris: No, I don't think we decide where it needs to be perfect—God has decided because he has given us the Scriptures and used people to preserve them in areas that are essential.

 BRIAN: Well, then, when you come into numerical differences or factual differences that are the same story in two different places, do we think that is due to interpretations and translations?

 DAD: I'll be honest: I haven't studied the specific instances that y'all are talking about. I haven't looked at what the scholars who believe that it is without error would say about that. And I don't claim to be a great theologian. I would say that my belief in the inerrancy of Scripture is based on faith, so I don't have any answers for this.

 CHRIS: But you could go through dozens of different stories in the Old Testament, where it's the same story, different number; same story, different city—so it's not that it's flawless, but it's not an important part of the story.

DAD: Again, I can't speak to that issue because I don't know the specific instances and I haven't studied those who are far better qualified to answer that. I really can't. I'm not sure it's worth anybody's time or effort to try to prove that there are inconsequential errors in Scripture. I'm not sure who is served by that.

CHRIS: But you don't have to spend much time to prove it. If you read the Old Testament stories, the discrepancies are there. So people who try to refute Scripture would point those out. When you make it an all-or-nothing thing, when you say there is nothing in Scripture that is wrong, then you set people up to say, "Well, here is one thing that's wrong, so now the whole thing is wrong." If I tell you the story of yesterday, and I say we were at your house but really we were at Pop's house— well, either way it's the same story. It's not an important fact in the story.

DAD: I understand what you are saying, and I will admit I am not qualified to debate the specific kinds of instances you are talking about. I will tell you that there are theologians who are far better qualified than any of us who in their minds have a way to reconcile those. And I don't see that as a point worth pursuing.

CHRIS: Dad, it's obvious that this conversation is frustrating for you—but we are not trying to debate, just to point some things out.

THE BIBLE: INERRANT OR AUTHORITATIVE?

As you can see, this is not a conversation my Dad wanted to have. He has spent his life studying the Scriptures but has always avoided the areas that might create tension with what he believes. In some ways I admire the fact that he holds to a childlike faith when it comes to the nature of Scripture. But I believe wrestling with these questions would not erode his respect and love for the Bible—I think it would make it stronger.

On a recent trip together, I asked my Dad to read through a few factual errors in the canon. We started with a gruesome story told twice in the book of Judges. In Judges 4, Jael kills Sisera in his sleep; in Judges 5, Sisera is standing and falls at her feet. In both accounts, she stabs him through the skull with a tent peg—clearly the same story. Which account is correct? Dad scratched his head and said, "I see what you're saying." My dad has studied the Scriptures for many years and holds three degrees, all of them from conservative institutions that are somehow afraid to consider the many factual disagreements in the Scriptures. They throw around words like *inerrant*, but they almost sound more Muslim than Christian in their description of Scripture. I love the Bible, and I believe it's perfect in every way it needs to be. But I serve a living God, not a canon.

Dad feels the acknowledgement of factual errors puts us on a slippery slope. I say we're already on a slippery slope; in the age of proof texting, people can make the Bible say anything they want it to anyway. Once the Scriptures were given to the church, the likelihood that we would misuse them was as sure as our nature is sinful. The real question is: Will we allow them to point us toward a living God?

As for navigating theological differences, I let most of them go—at least the ones that are really more about power than about truth. And most of them—let's not kid ourselves—are about power and not truth. I believe it's possible for people to have bad theology and still know Christ. And while my job as their pastor may be to lead them to Christ and to maturity, I am certainly not going to take a noisy stand against their position, showing impatience, showing judgment, and causing division. How would that be fulfilling the desires of Christ's prayer in John 17? To me, it's not a black-and-white issue. If I don't take a stand on an issue, that doesn't mean I support the opposition—it just means I'm choosing not to fight this battle.

The primary issue may be about having a missional heart. A missional pastor may say, "Look, the important thing here is that people come to know Christ, not that we argue as God's children." Scripture says we are to agree with one another. I take this to mean we should put aside our petty differences on small issues. But on the flip side, Paul stood up to Peter regarding eating with Gentiles. To Paul, this was an issue worth fighting about. It seems issues worth fighting about, then, are issues concerning reaching people for Christ. How far have we come from that heart? Nowadays, people who don't know the redemption that is found only in Christ aren't even on the radar, so we just fight with each other.

CHAPTER 6

WHEN I REALIZED PASTORS ARE SOMETIMES ARROGANT JERKS

How a Pastor Survives Destructive Criticism

I spent 10 years in Waco, Texas, which should be more than enough for any man. When it comes to times and events, my memory is poor. My brain is like a bowl of alphabet soup, that is, mostly indistinguishable except for rare occasions that are recorded complete with visual, audio, and even scent. It's as though my life is full of generic gaps with some indelible snapshots thrown in the mix. Waco memories go something like this: I move into my dorm at Baylor; I make friends; I enjoy my classes; I join a fraternity; I pastor a rural church; blah, blah, blah. Then one day after class, I notice the perfectly clear sky is tainted by puffs of dark smoke in the distance, and CNN confirms my worst fear: the Davidian standoff had ended and the smoke in the sky was filled with the remains of innocent women and children. That day was painful for our entire nation as we joined together in mourning around boxes of light and sound tuned to CNN. But those of us who saw the smoke simultaneously through the television and through our windows, will never forget it.

I met a friend named David Crowder. In January 1995, we started University Baptist Church, and I found out that my calling made sense. In only six weeks of existence, the church exploded from 0 to 600. We were telling the story of God in a way that it made sense. One month later, a local pastor wrote a scathing article in his church newsletter defaming both my church and me. I had never even met the man. Assuming there must be a misunderstanding, I called him at his office. The same man who had stood behind a pulpit the day before uttered pure vile and arrogance through the phone lines, "Son, we are in a different class—you don't amount to s**t and you never will. Maybe you will make me eat my words. But I doubt it." The words are forever imprinted in my brain. *Good to visit with you, Pastor.* What do you say to that? He wasn't even worth my sarcasm. Sometimes I think about calling him and rattling off my accomplishments or sharing with him how Phillip Yancey or Calvin Miller read one of my books and liked it. But, sanity returns and I decide I'll just send him a copy of this book with a clever comment inscribed on the signature page. Never mind, I won't do that either.

PLAYING OFFENSE

I am amazed by how many jerks there are in the pulpit. Catholics need to rid the clergy of pedophiles; and Protestants need to run off a lot of arrogant morons who see the church as a means to build up their egos. As this middle-aged, supercilious minister berated me on the phone, I was simultaneously humiliated and angry. I look back now and realize I adopted a new posture after that day—my wit was sharper, my attitude jaded, and I was more skeptical about a group of Boomer pastors who seemed to love and hate me at the same time. My ideas were cementing into dogma and without knowing it, I was becoming the very things I hated in others.

In retrospect, I realize I spent a number of years guarding myself from this kind of pain, and I am sad to say I went on the offense. Sometimes it was with fundamentalists who exposed their profound trust in science and psychology while professing the "Bible Alone." But mostly it was with the Church Growth Gang who perfected the art of slick. Centuries of Christian worship experiences were condensed to a 60-minute, glitch-free presentation. In the late 1990s, I did my best to convince them of their foolishness. I insulted their mullet hairstyles, mocked their booty-shaking pianist, and snubbed their band-in-a-box called the midi. They stood their ground seemingly undeterred. The wings of their hair grew fluffier, the pastels grew brighter, and soon the entire throng of miked vocalists began to shake their own booties. This was a war I couldn't win. People—large crowds of people—actually enjoyed this contemporary worship shenanigan. Who was I to rob them of such joy? So I gave up the culture wars. My battle between Eddie Vedder and Barry Manilow had ended. If they don't mind our worship sounding a bit like Wilco or Coldplay, then theirs can relive the glory days of Neil Diamond with electronic drums and sequined shirts. I look back on many experiences and realize I failed at being a peacemaker, at building bridges, at making friends, and at being a blessing to others. I deeply regret it.

The transition I'm walking through now is much more about substance than style. I pray that with additional years I'll have more patience and grace. The gospel is always about uniting us amidst our diversity. I knew that in my head, but it seems like it's the easiest thing to forget. Ministry puts you on the front line—ready to take the hits. It's exhausting sometimes.

PLAYING DEFENSE

 ROBBIE: It seems like one of the main things I'd like to hear you talk about (to *Papa*) is the idea of longevity and continuity, because in modern-day ministry, nobody stays at a church as long as you did. [It's] one of the most commendable things when we look back on your ministry, because so many pastors' families move and move and it never stops. Were there any times when you just wanted to bail—you know, I mean, just start somewhere fresh? Those that don't leave seem to burn out in a blaze of glory. How did that not happen to you Pop?

 PAPA: Well probably the last five years at Mangum Oaks/Inwood Forest I had what they call burnout. I was really just ready to jump ship. There was some mornings when I got up to preach and I just dreaded it, not because I didn't want to preach, but because I was feeling that burnout [that] I don't think [I felt] any other place. Now, I had some rough times at some other churches. Grace Memorial B.C. on the south side of Houston—I had a rough year there that just wasn't the best in the world. But I stayed with it until Mangum Oaks called me, and I felt...Betty and I drove around Oak Forest, Garden Oaks, Mangum Manor, all those places down there and we said this is where God wants us. And I made the statement when we were down there, "Wow wouldn't it be great if God just let us retire here?", never thinking something like that would happen. But he called, it happened, and we had a great ministry there. We had some good times, we had some good people, and we had some hard times; but the good times far outweighed the bad times.

 CHRIS: Okay, Pop. This is part of what Robbie is asking too—you are a pastor, you are an open target for criticism, and that's what you get. Like right now, I have this guy—an angry, middle-aged man—doing background searches on me. Every time he walks in the room, I'm an open target. Most people get enough of that and they are done, you're ready to get out of there. It's probably part of the reason [why] most pastors leave after about two years. How do you push through that year after year and find purpose in the midst of people's ugliness?

 PAPA: Well, I never had that 'cause I was such a good guy. In the first two churches I had no difficulties, no problems; I didn't know what it meant. I remember so many telling me different ways I was going to find trouble in church. The New Testament professor at Decatur, which is now Dallas Baptist College, told me every preacher somewhere in his ministry has to go through the baptism of fire, and I didn't know what that meant because I didn't go through that until I went to Grace Memorial Baptist Church. I had a few slight difficulties there, and I didn't know that deacons could be so mean and so troublesome until I got out of there. I wanted to get out of it; I wanted to quit because I didn't know ministry was going to be like that. There was one deacon...he picked [on] little things. Betty had never experienced anything like this. His wife would come over to the parsonage—this was our experience with a parsonage—she would walk in the house and would rub her hands across the top of the refrigerator and the furniture. If there was any dust on her hands, she would just [chew Betty] out because she wasn't keeping the parsonage clean. We had that; and sometimes it was the preaching was too rough, too long, and not long enough. Those things just got you down in a hole somewhere and you thought you just couldn't get out. At Mangum Oaks, I never really had this. Now I had some difficulties at Grace Memorial, which I think every pastor has somewhere in his ministry. I was also told that two things would get you in trouble in ministry if you didn't watch it: money and women. And I didn't have to worry about money because I didn't have any; but I found out that wasn't what they were talking about.

IT'S HOW YOU PLAY THE GAME

Trouble comes and goes. If peace, fame, and recognition are your motivators for the work you do—it's going to be a long ride. I returned recently to University Baptist Church in Waco to celebrate the church's 10th anniversary. Looking back at those who came to faith in that place and struggled through the challenging questions of what it means to walk in the way of Christ gave me a sense of rare satisfaction. If I was smart, I would save all the e-mails and notes that remind me that hours of sermon preparation, hospital visits, counseling, writing, and oversight is worth all the trouble that accompanies those things. For every good memory, there were bad ones at their heels: stalkers, haters, death, broken relationships, firing employees, being betrayed by people you love. The truth is those challenges sometimes jaded me and other times they refined my character. But I never succeeded in escaping them—they changed me.

CHAPTER 7

GOVERNMENT AND POLITICS

How a Pastor Navigates the Political Landscape

I like to discuss all kind of subjects with great veracity. There are only a few subjects I avoid in routine conversation: professional wrestling, the artistic contributions of Neil Diamond (Mom's a huge fan), and abortion. Let's talk about fried food, colonics, magnet therapy, or the percentage of the Gross National Product derived from men's hair products—but to address the polarizing question of abortion is painful, at best. This is not the kind of thing you bring up during a haircut or with a stranger on an airplane. But there are few issues more pressing for people of faith.

Abortion is the real difference between the red and blue states, in my opinion. If Kerry or Gore had cracked the door to potential pro-life cabinet members and justices, they could have been sleeping at 1600 Pennsylvania Avenue.

I believe we are all for life—only a few nut jobs would actually say they are for death. So the question becomes, "When does life begin?" I know the majority of readers are gasping now, some of them even angry that I would bring up the question. But this is the important question, and if we can't respond to this question without gasping or getting angry, nobody—*nobody*—will listen to a pro-life argument. And if nobody will listen, many lives will be lost. In short, gasping and getting angry is the most terrible thing we can do if we want to save lives.

Regarding the question about when life begins, there are a few options. They range from conception to the first breath. We must consider these ideas authentically and openly and seek a peaceful and reasoned dialogue. Our culture should quit talking through bumper stickers and protest signs and sit down together and listen—the argument, in fact, is quite compelling.

We talked about this at the table and the conversation got heated. I'd asked Don Miller to join us again, and he and my dad got a bit tense. They love each other very much, but—well, you'll see...

WHAT DOES IT REALLY MEAN TO BE PRO-LIFE?

 DAD: I don't want to be offensive to you, Don. But it's a struggle for me as a Christian to hear anyone say, as a Christian, that they would support the Democratic Party, though I agree with them on a wide range of issues. But to me—and you may shoot down this analogy if you want to—slavery was a pivotal moral issue of an earlier era. In my heart, abortion is the pivotal moral issue in our generation. To me, I don't care what else they are for that may be right—if they are for the murder of defenseless babies in the womb, then I could never support them.

 ROBBIE: I think the bigger question there is: Are they for the government interaction?

 BRIAN: There are a lot of Republicans who are pro-life who aren't willing to do anything about it.

 DON MILLER: We have a Republican president right now, and women can still get abortions. Is he failing? Let's not assume that if you vote Republican you are saving the lives of unborn children. The truth is—as hard as it is to hear—if you vote Republican, you are voting with somebody who is pro-life but with limited resources to make considerable changes. Contrast that with the lives lost in Africa and in the third world, by our neglect there, and you have to start counting bodies—unborn bodies versus African bodies. Would you concede that if the body count is higher because of Republican interest in corporate America over third world politics, then our moral obligation is to vote for the lesser of two evils?

 BRIAN: I think this is where we can find common ground, in the sense that this is not trying to legislate morality for the sake of morality—you are stepping in for people who cannot step in for themselves. To me, that is the difference. That's where it is the church's responsibility within the government and outside the government to begin to fight for that issue.

 ROBBIE: I think you and Chris and I stand a little more liberal than our father—does that make sense that you would never vote against the rights of the unborn?

 BRIAN: It makes sense, yes.

 DON MILLER: I think there are two issues here: one is that there were many, many fewer abortions under Clinton than there have been under [George W.] Bush. When you take people's freedom, they tend to rebel against that loss of freedom. Same with teen pregnancy, same with crime...and these are not related to economic conditions. So a vote for a Democrat does not mean a vote for people to be able to have abortions. Reagan wasn't able to stop abortions; Bush isn't going to be able to stop abortions. So you have to look at it like that, which is incredibly hard for an evangelical Republican. I can sit down and show them actual statistics, and the evangelical Republicans will literally keep voting so that *more* people die, just because they are voting on an issue, not on the basis of statistics. It's crazy. This goes back to that missional mindset. One of the reasons I joined the Democratic Party was that I had met so many Democrats. I had embedded myself in a lost culture and wanted to say, look, we have things in common, we are not that different, we care about humanitarian issues, we care about social justice, we care about Africa, India, the Middle East, and Latin America—so much so that I began to say, "Man, this is a mixed bag." And I saw the Republicans neglect the poor and favor the rich, not just abroad but at home. My mom lost 95 percent of her retirement when Enron collapsed; those were Republicans who did that, and I said these guys are criminals and thieves. She heated her bathwater on the stove, and George W. Bush denied he knew Ken Lay. Denied it. He lied. So for me, it is both: It's the fact that if I vote for a Republican, certain people will lose their lives, there is no doubt about it; and if I vote for a Democrat, certain other people will lose their lives. However, if I choose the Democratic Party, without question it helps me reach the lost; and if I don't, it isolates me within the group of people I deal with. Let's not pretend there is a "good party" and a "bad party." That is a lie from Satan. Both are trying to do good things, and both have ugly sides.

 ROBBIE: But I just don't like the argument that if we look the other way that perhaps it will happen less, maybe we don't take a stand and it will happen less.

 DAD: I don't see the parallel. I don't think Clinton deserves any credit.

 ROBBIE: I agree that it doesn't necessarily mean there are going to be more abortions, but that's like saying let's not voice our opinion and just hope it happens less.

 CHRIS: But I think that puts it back on our plate. My hope that the government is going to substantially fix any of these problems is pretty low. I mean, does it factor into the way I vote? Yeah. It becomes a big part of it. I mean, I watched my daughter come out, in the water, not having yet breathed with her mouth but looking at me, and the thought of someone saying that she was not yet alive and could be killed at that point is unbelievable to me because I held Trinity. But the people dying in the Sudan—we've got to figure it out. These babies are dying, and these other people are dying, and there are no clear choices anymore. Bush says he is for life. Well, he is for life in some areas and is for death and violence in other places. I don't know how to calculate who is more for life and who is less for life, I know there aren't many who are really, really for life, and I hope one day the church stands up for the unborn babies, for children in Southeast Asia, and for the refugees in the Sudan and in other places and says, "You know, this has got to stop." And I don't fully know how to do that.

 DAD: I would agree. It's not an either/or; it's a both/and.

 CHRIS: And that's where people like James Dobson need to be working in those areas that are issues of justice more than personal morality. Dobson is supporting an ultrasound program that Mom *(my mother is an RN who works at a Crisis Pregnancy Center)* can use to show mothers what their babies look like. I love that. He is going to buy those machines. He's obviously got the ability to raise a lot of money, and he buys a lot of other things. That's about justice to me. Now, some of the other things he says on TV and radio sometimes prompts people toward hatred and violence toward other people. It really bothers me. It makes me wonder if he is taking a stand for justice or taking a stand for morality, and the motives are different—very different. It's not that morality isn't good—but justice is about saving lives, while morality is about behavior.

 DAD: Well, perhaps, but I think you can always find fault with any leader because he is certainly a fallible man, as we all are. So I think it's not so much that we should criticize him because he is only involved in this area to the neglect of other areas. You know, pray that God raises up champions in these other areas.

FLAGSHIP ISSUES

 CHRIS: What Brian is saying is really important: if we focus on justice, this requires something of us. The reality is that there are people in our families, in our churches, people we are close to [who live in moral failure of some kind and] we just tend to ignore those things and not deal with them. [The fight against immorality is a losing battle—we are better off if we focus on justice.]

 DAD: Well, it depends on what you mean by that. I think to love people unconditionally is not ignoring that.

 DON MILLER: On this issue, I have been trying to answer this question for the last two years, and as I've been listening to Christian radio here in Houston—

 ROBBIE: It's great, isn't it?

 DON MILLER: Yeah, it is. When the newsbreak happens, there are two topics that are always covered: gay marriage and abortion. These are the only two issues that Republicans care about that Jesus cares about. Trickle-down economics is not a Jesus issue, nor is George Gilder economics a Jesus issue—it's wrong, it's sin. Reaganomics is sin in the eyes of God, I am convinced of that. So we've got these two issues that the Republicans care about, so they'll throw us a bone on these two issues. As I look at the Democratic Party and the Republican Party, I look at abortion and I think the issue of abortion does not belong in the Republican Party. The pro-life agenda belongs in the Democratic Party because it appreciates the sanctity of human life. And I look at the Republican Party and I think there isn't a whole lot of appreciation of the sanctity of human life in this party, except for the abortion issue. And I mean that. Objectively, as I look at it, these are not people who care about all of humanity; they care about making more money. And that is true of a lot of Democratic leaders, too, but how did the Republican Party get associated with hatred? The Democratic Party is not associated with hatred at all. Why? I think part of it is this concern for all of humanity. Clinton negotiated the price of drugs in Africa for AIDS patients from $112 to 37 cents. Bush isn't allowing that to happen because he is a businessman and he says, "The pharmaceutical companies designed these drugs and they deserve to sell them for $112. We are not going to interfere." And I just have serious questions about that. And so I side with Democrats on that issue. And then I come to abortion and I'm with the Republicans on that. And as I listen to the news and then the Christian news, I think gay marriage and abortion are the two issues they talk about because those are the only issues they can talk about and still support a Republican agenda. They can't talk about Africa, the United Nations, the World Bank, the welfare state, single moms, Equal Opportunity, education, migrant workers, none of it. Christian radio can only support the Republican position on those two issues.

DAD: Well perhaps so. Those are definitely the hot button issues.

DON MILLER: Why? Why?

DAD: Right or wrong, I think there are issues that come to the forefront as the seminal issues of any generation, and I think that for most Christians, those are the issues. I would again draw the parallel to slavery; of all the other moral and legislative bills of that era, slavery dwarfed them because of its hideous nature. I think abortion is of that magnitude in the minds of other believers, and certainly in my mind. I would not disagree with any of the issues you have raised. On gun control, I am totally in agreement with the Democratic Party, and there are other issues.

 CHRIS: Death penalty...Democratic Party.

 DAD: There are other issues where I feel more akin to their position, but again...what if slavery was the issue? I think there are many Christians who just have not yet grasped the moral magnitude of the abortion issue.

 BRIAN: Where the Democratic Party has completely failed is that there is no openness to a Democrat who is pro-life.

 DON MILLER: They are ostracized. It isn't good. I hate that about the Democratic Party. It confuses me about them. I don't know why they won't support an unborn child. It doesn't fit their platform at all. I wish they could see it.

 BRIAN: As a party platform, Jim Wallis wrote an article in *Sojourners* a couple of months ago that basically outlined that the Republican Party has done a better job of saying, "You want to be pro-choice and a Republican, we can live with that, you have the right to do that, we'll still let you speak, and you can still be a part of the Republican Party." But with the Democrats, if you are pro-life, if your organization is pro-life—they will not link you to the Democratic National Party Web site.

 DON MILLER: And here is why: it's because the pro-life agenda is not a pillar of the Republican Party. Evangelicals think it is, but it isn't; it is a bone.

DAD: They would disagree with that; they look at it as a plank in the platform. But think of this: when I was growing up and when Pop was growing up, almost all evangelical Christians were Democrats. And if you take those two major issues and you switch them, then the Democratic Party becomes the pro-life party, and they become the ones who assure no loss of religious freedom. I'll say that the gay marriage issue is not going to impact the freedoms of people of faith, so that if you were to switch those, there would be a mass movement.

DON MILLER: There would be.

DAD: A movement back to the Democratic Party. Eh, but here's my flagship issue.

BRIAN: Here's where I would disagree with that statement: we are too comfortable as Americans with our big American dream, individualism, money, big government, making a lot of money...

DAD: Wealthy Christians.

BRIAN: We are all wealthy Christians; we're too comfortable even when we are not wealthy. The potential to be wealthy is still there, and so I wonder if abortion is really the hinge issue...

CHRIS: I would hope it is.

DAD: For the people who listen to Christian radio, I really think it is, and that's why they do that.

DOBSON, FALWELL, AND HAGEE

 DON MILLER: With millions of people—millions of Christians—dying in the Sudan because of their faith, and millions more in Rwanda—what, six years ago, 10 years ago—it never got any play on Christian radio. You know, we are just three percent of the people that God made. Three percent live in this country; this is ridiculous. We are part of such a tiny sliver of the kingdom of God, so small. Our brothers and sisters are dying, and we are ignoring them.

 DAD: Well, that is where I think it's going to take God raising up people with a passion for that issue and various other issues.

 DON MILLER: And there are people with that passion. I mean, the mission organizations that your generation basically started are just unbelievable. I mean, who could ask for more? But they are not political issues, they are missional issues. Honestly, I want to say this—because I think our conversation is going to switch—as an apology in advance for such strong statements about James Dobson. I do feel licensed with two people—three: James Dobson, John Hagee, and Jerry Falwell—to make statements that are that harsh, only because those three make statements about lost people that are that harsh. They are not polite. They have said unkind and angry things.

 DAD: I would agree with Falwell and Hagee, but I have not heard...

 DON MILLER: Dobson has softened in the last 10 years. He is a good man. I know he is a good man. I wish he knew the damage he causes when he uses the war metaphor, when he says we are at war with homosexuals. Meanwhile, Muslims are beheading people in their holy war. That seems like a bad move to me, to use war imagery.

 DON MILLER: I met with the vice-president of Thomas Nelson, and I made some very strong statements about John Hagee. The vice president looked at me and said, "He's my best friend, he counseled me through my divorce, he's like a father to me." And I said, "I am so sorry. Please forgive me. Sometimes people come off as angry and bitter, but are kind and altruistic in person."

 CHRIS: I think we are trying to figure out who we are talking to. I mean, this is a conversation that we have amongst ourselves and in the church, and Dobson and Falwell don't spend a lot of time thinking about who they are talking to. But I think Jesus was a perfect model of that, knowing who he was speaking to and knowing who to love and who to rebuke. We end up rebuking the people we love and loving the people we should rebuke, and until that changes...

SLAVERY, CIVIL RIGHTS, AND CHRISTIAN ACTION

 ROBBIE: Back on the political topic, I think the Republicans and Democrats have one thing in common, and that's money, more than anything. The economy is the number one issue, so money is everything...

 DAD: Both sides will say anything to stay in power.

 BRIAN: I wonder if the Mennonites have it right, if they've got it figured out. They say, "We are just not going to mess with that stuff. We are going to figure out ways to deal with those issues in our church and community."

DAD: But I think that if we took that stance, the generations to come would be saying what Chris said about the Christians during slavery—"Where were those Christians?"

 BRIAN: Those churches still stood up for those issues without feeling like legislation was the answer. I'm not sure that Mennonite is the way to go, but I think they would say, "We still fight for those issues, we fight for them vehemently, and we create things in our community that fight for those issues. We go after plantation owners, but we just don't think that legislation and arguing about politics is the way we are going to redeem the world."

 PAPA: You don't think they fought against slavery? The church, that is?

 CHRIS: The church—I mean, it's still the most segregated place in America. The church has been the one on the back end of the civil rights movement.

 BRIAN: In Martin Luther King Jr.'s autobiography, he said the most disappointing and surprising thing was the resistance from white pastors to support what he was doing and to acknowledge that what he was doing was a justice issue and about saving people. He said that what he got instead of support were letters telling him to "quit breaking the law" and how he should be a better boy and take better care of himself and his people. So my response, from what I read in history books, is no—I don't think the church as a whole fought against slavery as they should have.

 PAPA: I don't think they fought at all.

BRIAN: But I think there were minority voice churches, like the Mennonites, that said, "We can't fix this through the government; we can fix this through the church and by reaching out to people around us."

 PAPA: I think if the church had fought for it, it might have been a lot different and a lot faster.

 CHRIS: And at least we'd be doing what's right. I think that is what Brian is saying, too: *I am going to do what is right, and if they come after me, then they come after me.* Instead we pansy around these things, and maybe we don't actually stand up for what is right.

 DAD: Just to add one postscript, I don't really think these leaders are under the illusion that this is going to redeem the culture. They think this is necessary to keep the moral fabric of the nation together.

 CHRIS: To protect themselves.

 DAD: To protect the whole country.

 BRIAN: If I were just a citizen opposed to homosexuality, then that could be my platform. But I say, as the church, that it is not our job to try to legislate morality. According to the gospel I read in Scripture, I get from Jesus that we are to be a radical community of people who are—regardless of what laws and legislation are going on around us—to live this Sermon on the Mount lifestyle. And if it is happening around us, then we are going to fight for these justice issues. But I read the New Testament and see that they didn't care that the emperor wanted to kill them; they just kept being the church. In Acts, when James is martyred and Paul is in prison and they let him out, they don't stop being the church or go after the emperor and try to convince him to be a Christian so they can stop being persecuted. It just says they kept on preaching, and thousands were added to their number daily.

 DON MILLER: And that's indicative of a switch from not having any power and being oppressed to where we are in America—once having had power and having lost that power.

 BRIAN: But we don't recognize that. We can't help but come at it from a different angle because since Constantine, at least in the Western sense, we have had the power. So we don't know what it's like to be powerless, and so we are afraid of that idea as well. We fight these issues out of fear because we think we won't truly be effective as a church if we don't have that power.

 CHRIS: Part of the beautiful thing about this and all the other theological things we'll get into is that we do have strong disagreement, but we agree on the essential parts of these things.

 DAD: Yeah, we agree that our mission—our primary mission—is to win people to faith and to disciple each other.

 CHRIS: So, to disagree on how we do that is a healthy and good thing.

 PAPA: I think we agree to disagree. I don't agree with what [you've] said, most of it. I just read what the Bible says, and that's the way I am going to go, whether anyone else agrees with me or not. You know, when you talk about homosexuality, the Bible says one man, one woman—and I'm not going any further than that.

CHRIS: I agree with that; we don't disagree on that. We just don't agree on whether it's about the church or the government.

 PAPA: It's not about either one. It's about your heart and where you are. I don't think we should legislate morality; it's not my place to say to you or another who is homosexual. The only thing I can say to you is that it's sin, and it's up to you to live the way you want to live. I don't think anyone can force you to be a Christian.

 BRIAN: That's what I was trying to say. He just said it.

 DAD: We look back on what the church did and didn't do during the rise of Nazi regime, and we see how negligent the church was as it chose to be silent and separate, and what a mistake that was. I don't think we are going to know what the right approach is until we can look back a couple of generations. I'm confident in what I think is right, and so are you.

 BRIAN: I think the sin of the German National Church was not that it was silent, but that it aligned itself with the government above the gospel; it aligned itself with a particular ideology instead of saying, "I know they are Jews and they don't believe in Christ, but I am still going to fight for their rights."

 DAD: Well, aligning is even a step further than silence.

 CHRIS: Dietrich Bonhoeffer had the courage and the conviction to be ready to attempt to kill Hitler.

 BRIAN: He was a pacifist, of course.

CHRIS: And you know, some of these nut jobs that I just can't stand, who kill abortionists—all of a sudden you compare them, and it makes you at least a little uncomfortable.

MAKE CHANGES WHEREVER YOU CAN

This was, perhaps, our most tense conversation. I don't know if the text reveals the stiffness in my dad or the frustration in Don's eyes or the silent wisdom of my grandfather. It reminded me that when the Fall happened, chaos happened. I think there are times I fall into thinking, *If we could just get this piece of legislation through*—or *If we could just side with these protestors*—or *If the church would just think this way, we would suddenly have a lot of peace and things would be good.* But it won't happen. Our King Jesus will come, and he will rule, and we will all be amazed at how well things work with him in charge.

But we stumble through this fallen world. I looked into my newborn daughter's eyes as she reached for me while still submerged in gentle waters, and I can tell you for sure that life had already begun. I wonder if my responsibility as a pastor involves, somehow, teaching the sanctity of human life to my neighbors, to the people who walk into my church. To say, "You are a human and you are beautiful." To say, "Look around: look at these gentle women, look at these wonderful children, look at these strong men who are my brothers and friends and believe with me in the sanctity of human life." In other words, maybe change starts very small, and while I may or may not be responsible for changing things on a government level, we know one thing for sure: I am responsible to change things at my church, in my neighborhood, in the hearts of those who look to me as their pastor.

CHAPTER 8

HOW TO MAKE MILLIONS OFF JESUS

How a Pastor Navigates Money Issues

I know home is where the heart is, so the three-bedroom home in the Inwood Forest neighborhood on Houston's north side will forever be home to me. It is the backdrop to my fondest memories of growing up. The structure is less than impressive. In fact, I am almost sure that in all the years we spent at my grandparents' house, we compared it unfavorably to the house across the street—the one with grand columns that drew comparisons to the White House or the mansion of my fourth grade classmate who had a skating rink in the backyard. (I never actually saw the inside of that house but often spoke of it as though I had.)

But like the sting of Peter Cetera's words (of Chicago rock ballad fame), "You don't know what you've got 'til it's gone." That simple house was warm and instantly intimate in a way that seemed magical. Hot summers were energized by the small L-shaped swimming pool. Countless hours were spent playing, lounging, and eating by the pool. Every December I go back there in my mind: the scent of Christmas candy, the clutter of infinite gifts, and a family room that, even with an enormous Christmas tree in the corner, could hold 30 people. I pray my home will offer my children and grandchildren a fraction of the joyous memories I knew there. If so, they will be truly blessed.

If I ever write a bestseller and have more money than I need to pay the bills, it's clear where the extra money will be spent. I have one persistent financial dream (besides retiring on a Mexican beach with unlimited guacamole y Corona): to buy back my grandparents' home at 4310 Birchcroft. My grandparents decided to move to a small house in the country to find a slower pace to life. The experiment was a failure from the start. The contractor hired to remodel the old home asked to be paid cash in advance. Because he was a deacon in the church, my grandfather obliged. Long story short—no work was done and their nest egg was gone. In declining health, they are now living on $800 a month in Social Security. How is it that two people who have modeled generosity so well—sharing whatever they had, historically giving over 20 percent of their income—are now at the mercy of the Social Security Administration? Pastoral ministry is not exactly lucrative. I sure hope Jesus wasn't kidding around about gaining all those riches in heaven. I'm not very fond of jewelry so the whole motivation to do the right thing so my crown will sparkle just doesn't work for me. (Although, I wonder if that metaphor is making a comeback in churches ministering in a hip-hop culture? I doubt it.)

As we dialogued about finances, I struggled to reconcile their economic reality. Don't people who serve the church faithfully for so many years deserve better than to barely get by on government checks? Tom Brokaw has called my grandparents' generation "The Greatest Generation," and I would have to agree with him. Just listening to my grandfather talk about the good years—about how his churches were growing, about thousands trying to get in to old gospel concerts—made me realize we have come a long way, and perhaps not in any great direction. It made me realize, as well, that back when people didn't have all the money we have these days—all the wonder of air-conditioning and dishwashers, all the conveniences—they had more, not less. They had more of each other, more need for their church, less need for television, more need for family.

We were all wondering how Papa and Noni felt about these changes, about what their lives had become, and about how their own financial situation hadn't ended up the way some of us thought it should have. We wondered if back then life was better than it is now. We wondered if they were angry, hurt, depressed. It's likely they had been all these things; but when we asked about life, then compared to now, and specifically about the financial side of things—we heard a faith-filled response.

MONEY IN THE CHURCH

 PAPA: I had somebody (and this is where I learned to never do this) walking out the church door one day, and they gave me their tithe. They forgot to put it in the plate, and they asked me to put it in. But I forgot, and I put it in my pocket; I found it in there about a month later—it was still there. The envelope hadn't been opened or anything, but from that point forward, I never did that again. As far as money, I never had any difficulties. No one ever accused me of taking money. I knew some other pastors who were accused and it was finally brought out that it happened. But, praise the Lord, I never had that situation.

 CHRIS: Part of it is that even though you guys weren't rich—you didn't have much money—you always gave more than the typical tithe.

 PAPA: We gave as the Lord directed us to give. When we came to Mangum Oaks, they had—I don't know—maybe 20 people; and my secretary and I were the only ones on staff there. I had five children and lots of bills, and they were only going to pay me $100 a week, but I never had any doubt that the Lord was going to take care of us, and he did. We never had a problem. Oh, we got a little hungry, but it was never a problem.

 CHRIS: And you turned around and put 10 dollars in the offering plate?

 PAPA: Well, I could tell you a lot of instances where the Lord blessed what we gave, how he returned it. It proves how that works; it's just something I learned a long time ago. In Mangum Oaks, about six months after we were there, we had to build. Then about a year and three months after that, we had to build again. And two years later we had to relocate because we had outgrown our building. We moved into Inwood Forest Elementary School for about a year and a half.

 DAD: I remember there was no air-conditioning. We ended up getting a truck, finally, to pump in some air-conditioning.

 PAPA: Back at that time they had trucks at the airport, and when a plane landed they put a big hose in the plane and shot air in there. We got one of those every Sunday in that school and put that hose in the window.

 ROBBIE: So if you sat close to that window, you were loving that...

 CHRIS: You remember how much that cost?

 PAPA: No, I don't. For today it wouldn't sound like much, but it was a pretty good price.

 DAD: But you needed something; I mean, it was so hot.

 CHRIS: You would preach for an hour and 10 minutes and...

 PAPA: You had to have something. I had a music minister at that time that just complained all the time. But it was a good time, it was a learning time; it was a time we enjoyed, kind of like FBC Magnolia now. We just got our educational space ready, so we moved into that, which was air-conditioned, and we had services in the fellowship hall for about a year. Not long after that, we built the gym, a college-size gym. Well, before we built the gym we started the school, Inwood Baptist School, the only Christian school in the area at the time, and it just grew by leaps and bounds. Then we built more educational space after that, for the school and the church. But the Lord blessed us while we were at Mangum Oaks.

 DAD: There was a time when that church was really growing.

 BRIAN: Some good kickball games in that gym.

 CHRIS: We used to roller-skate in there, remember that?

 PAPA: We opened that gym with the queen of the Grand Ole Opry, what was her name?

 CHRIS: Patsy Cline?

 PAPA: No, not Patsy Cline. It was one who was just as popular.

 DAD: Wanda Jackson.

 PAPA: Yeah, it was Wanda Jackson.

 ROBBIE: So, did she sing some tunes? Some gospel songs?

 DAD: Yeah, she's like a local Loretta Lynn.

 PAPA: She was a good Christian.

DAD: Big draw, too...

 PAPA: We had to turn people away. It was during that week of the grand opening, and the fire marshals came in there and said, "Uh-uh." We had some good times and a few bad times, but the good times far outweighed the bad times.

 CHRIS: Yeah, and we probably all tell those stories because that was home for us. Now...how did Noni handle those hard years?

 PAPA: Better than I.

 CHRIS: You never had the sense that she was giving up?

 PAPA: Oh no. She would never have done that.

 ROBBIE: Pop, you fall just behind what historians call the greatest generation that has ever lived in this country—you are on the tail end of that. Was there a different spirit in the men and women of that generation?

 PAPA: I think there was a tremendous difference in how that generation felt, and part of it was the loyalty to their nation. You know, when they bombed Pearl Harbor, the next day there were lines at recruiting stations to sign up. When they went into the World Trade Center, very few went to sign up; people don't have that built-in loyalty they used to have, even though now the government says they'll never have to have a draft because the volunteer army is so huge.

ROBBIE: I read a lot of history books, and I get the sense that maybe we are just spoiled on the fruits of the labor of generations past.

 CHRIS: We've come a long way economically since the time you were born. The things you probably enjoyed, we take for granted. What's the biggest difference between the world you grew up in and the world you live in now?

 PAPA: Air-conditioning.

 BRIAN: Don't have to bring in the truck from the airport?

 PAPA: Well, I lived in the country, and there was a difference there in the generation who went to church and those that didn't. Back then, the Church of Christ [members] were the only ones going to heaven, and the Baptists were going to hell. And back then, the Baptists and Methodists and a lot of them shouted and raised their hands and praised the Lord—in those days that was praise and worship. And they just died off as far as worship is concerned. We came to the traditional: you sing this song and this song and you go home. It's hard to say how much of a difference there was.

 CHRIS: But we are rich according to those standards.

 PAPA: Oh, I didn't have a dime and I was rich. I went to Mangum Oaks making $100 a week and I had a $50 light bill and a $25 gas bill, and car payments, and food for seven mouths, and not one time did we ever go hungry, or did we ever hurt for anything. I've never been poor in comparison to poor people, people that had a real need.

CHRIS: It's not that you never had a lot of money, but what you did have you spent on us as a family. So for us, it felt like, wow, there are a lot of gifts here; we had some really great Christmases. You guys got a little chunk of money, and you could have done a lot of things with it. But you put in that pool, and ultimately you didn't have money in the bank. You didn't have money sitting around anywhere, but what you did have you spent on us.

 ROBBIE: That is a small part of the legacy you leave us. We all spend our money on family; Dad spends all of his money on family. That's what we do because that's how it was growing up.

 DAD: Well, those are the values you were taught. I mean, the whole playground and all this stuff here *(at Mom and Dad's new house)* is out of that core value. I think that's where a lot of ministers' families get screwed up.

 PAPA: You know, I think it's wanting to do things for your grandkids that you didn't get to do for your own kids.

 BRIAN: Begs the question: When is the pool going in?

 ROBBIE: As soon as Brian builds it.

BEING RICH

These kids are blessed, not just with playgrounds, tree houses, and pools, but also with a family who actually loves being together. We really have a great time together (until somebody brings up James Dobson's name, and then things get a little ugly).

Since I wrote the first part of this chapter about my dream of buying my grandparents' home and giving it back to them, the dream has come true. No bestseller, yet. But my family has come together to live out the essence of Christ to the people who have given us the most. Papa is very weak—the man who stood behind a pulpit every Sunday for almost 50 years often falls in his own home. He is not currently capable of earning a regular paycheck or maintaining a house in the country. Ironically, that house was a place he bought for his mother. My great-grandmother had been widowed, and he wanted her to be close to her extended family, so he purchased a house and an acre for her personal residence. Three years after her death, it became their retirement home.

Now it was time for the following generations to reciprocate. In July 2004, our family came together to purchase my grandparents the first new home they have ever lived in. They live in a beautiful, custom three-bedroom home that sits on an acre (right next to my parents' home) and their children and grandchildren are paying for it. After a lifetime of ministry, they deserve the best we can give them. If you are in Magnolia, Texas, come by the house. Noni will pour you a cup of coffee and you can hear a few more stories—stories about how life used to be, about how hardship creates strength, and how families come together.

CHAPTER 9

SOCIAL ISSUES

Homosexuality and the Moral Society—
How a Pastor Navigates Social Tension

I was driving to the Phoenix airport on September 11, when tragedy struck our country. The cross-country drive home was laced with horrific anticipation that more tragedy was around the corner. I wondered about Islam, about terrorism. But before I could muster any kind of judgment, I remembered that the faith I subscribe to, Christianity, had historically been involved in equal acts of horror. Islam is not the only religion to produce hateful manifestations. Christianity bears the scars of the Crusades, the Holocaust, slavery, prejudice, and, it seems, a continued hostility to culture as a whole. It is difficult to imagine a Christianity that isn't against something and doesn't, at least in ignorant pockets, produce violent acts out of its "stand on truth." Watching Christian leaders speak on television feels like a full-contact sport. When they start talking, I feel like I've just been kicked in the gut.

Damage was done to the name of Jesus when Jerry Falwell went on *The 700 Club* and doused the television audience with salt, saying, "God continues to lift the curtain and allow the enemies of America to give us probably what we deserve. The American Civil Liberties Union has got to take a lot of blame for this." Then Falwell broadened his blast to include the federal courts and others who, he said, were "throwing God out of the public square." He added, "The abortionists have got to bear some burden for this because God will not be mocked. And when we destroy 40 million little innocent babies, we make God mad. I really believe that the pagans, and the abortionists, and the feminists, and the gays and the lesbians who are actively trying to make that an alternative lifestyle, the ACLU, People for the American Way—all of them who have tried to secularize America—I point the finger in their face and say, 'You helped this happen.'"[1] This comment was designed solely to produce anger, judgment, and hatred in anybody ignorant enough to believe such blanket, generic statements. The same seed that Jesus violently rebuked in the gospels is still producing the same tree and the same fruit, and one need look no further than any televangelist interviewed on CNN to see a man

Hmm

who does not love his enemies. Why do we tolerate this kind of disobedience while we are fighting immorality? What is the difference?

During a protest over insurance for partners of gay city employees, Pastor Artie Bucco looked straight into the Fox News camera and said, "Sodomites should have 'em an island. They got plenty of money—they ought to buy 'em an island and every sodomite ought to go out there to that island and just stay there. And maybe we can drop 'em a little food if they don't know how to grow their own food." I called him the following week at his church to see if his comments were taken out of context or he somehow misspoke. I asked him if this was his actual statement, and Pastor Bucco wanted it to be perfectly clear that the news segment had left something out. In his plan, those sodomites would have to pay for any food we dropped to them ("They don't get no charity."). Then Pastor Bucco of Grace (how ironic) Church informed me that the Bible calls sodomy an abomination, and Asa removed all sodomites from the community. When asked about the importance of living under the Hebrew Law of the Old Testament, he said, "We must live under the whole law!"

After further questioning, Bucco confessed to wearing a shirt made of two different kinds of thread, in his case a blend of cotton and polyester (mostly polyester), which is expressly forbidden in Leviticus 19:19. He also makes a habit of shaking the hands of women without asking if they are currently menstruating (Leviticus 15:19-24), a flagrant violation of the law. Furthermore, he partakes of shellfish of all kinds: barbecued shrimp, teriyaki shrimp, coconut shrimp, Creole shrimp, fried shrimp, and even shrimp salad, which the Old Testament considers an abomination, requiring that he be stoned to death. I asked him if we could set an appointment for his stoning. In seeing his

<hr>

[1] http://www.washingtonpost.com/ac2/wp-dyn?pagename=article&node=&contentId=A12100-2001Sep14&notFound=true

own transgressions, Pastor Bucco jested that stoning would soon have to become a regular event in his congregation.

This is the beauty of the new story found in Christ. We all ought to be stoned, but we have been shown grace. Could we try offering some grace to others? One of the great tragedies and ugly realities of the church is that we put the hot hand of discipline and anger on the world and not on the unrepentant church leaders who do not love their enemies. It's no wonder evangelical Christians are hated and despised by so many. My dad and grandfather can be pretty conservative, so conversations that involve the words *moral majority, Falwell,* and *Dobson* get interesting very quickly.

LOVING HOMOSEXUALS

 PAPA: Do we hate homosexuals, or do we love them?

 CHRIS: Well, I hope...I hope we love them.

 PAPA: I think you can see in the churches today that they don't love homosexuals.

 DON MILLER: Well, I think they ignore homosexuals. They don't know what to do with them.

 PAPA: Well, they're afraid to touch them, or have anything to do with them. That's like the blacks before the civil rights movement—white people were afraid it would rub off on them.

  DON MILLER: It's that, but it's also that we don't like the idea of telling people they are wrong, perhaps, so we ignore the issue. I mean, there are definitely church people who hate gays, but I don't think that is the case for most people. Most church people just don't want to deal with the issue, other than with their votes.

 PAPA: Well, before I left the church *(in the early 1980s)*, I brought up the idea of beginning something in the church to work with and help people with HIV, and I had two deacons hit the ceiling and say, "Absolutely not. We will not have anything to do with those people, or that type of a disease. That is their fault; they put it there; they brought it on themselves." We had some people who wanted to bring in people with HIV and teach them, work with them within the church, but the deacons would not allow it. Now, one of those deacons opposing it—he died not long after that.

 CHRIS: That's probably why he died.

 PAPA: Well, I didn't say that, but...

 CHRIS: What's his name? We can get him in there. We'll dedicate the book to him: *the guy who died because he hated gay people.*

 DAD: I don't think it's so much that we don't want to tell people they are wrong, but that we don't know *how* to tell people they are wrong in a compassionate and redemptive way. It's just easier to point the finger. I have spent some time preaching on the whole gay marriage issue and what it means culturally, legally, etcetera, and how we have to frame that with how to relate to homosexuals. A few years ago a homosexual couple began attending our church, and our people were very loving and open. Well, most of them were—there were a couple that weren't. Then they called and said, "You know, we never had such an accepting and loving group as your church.

We are going to come forward and join the church next Sunday." And I said, "We want you to, but let me explain to you our theology." And we basically talked about salvation and repentance and that homosexuality is no more condemnatory than any other sin, but that you have to repent of sin to accept redemption. And in the end, they were unwilling to confess their sin. And that's a difficult tension of trying to be loving and compassionate, yet at some point drawing the line and standing on truth. And some have the idea that you have to compromise truth to be compassionate, and that's not right, either.

COMPARING SINS

CHRIS: The challenge is that we have all these other areas where people come in clearly in sin, but we don't deal with those in the same way. We don't say to fat people, "Get yourself trimmed up and then we'll let you join the church." Should they publicly repent of gluttony and the love of chocolate before they can join the church?

DAD: But there is a list of sins in the Scriptures that says, "Don't be fooled...adulterers and swindlers," you know the passage. I think it means there are certain sins that are so obvious that if they are habitually present and practiced in a person's life, it indicates a lack of repentance.

CHRIS: But wouldn't gossip and all those other things be the same kind of thing?

DON MILLER: And Paul, when he is talking to the Jews and he's trying to say salvation through grace isn't some new liberal fix, always mentions sex and marriage. He says, "I defended the law, I defended this and this, and I defended sex and marriage," and sex is a different kind of thing for some reason. It's a sin of "oneness" more than many other sins. It's not that it is worse, but if salvation is relational, through Christ, then we can't go messing around with oneness.

DAD: Well, he says that all other sins are outside the body. And it's not necessarily that it is worse; it's just more easily identifiable.

DON MILLER: Is it because it is relational?

DAD: I think so; I think it goes to the most intimate personal dimension of a human being. I think a person can struggle with homosexual acts and fall into that sin, but what's important is an attitude of repentance toward it. What is repentance? It's looking at sin like God looks at sin. With a gambler, or an alcoholic, or someone caught looking at pornography, or gossip, or any other sin...if a person continually falls into it but seeks to come out of it by God's power, there can be repentance. But if a person says, "I don't care what the Bible says, I don't care what God expects, I'm hanging onto this," that's something else.

BRIAN: I guess my issue with homosexuality is that we have categorized sin, and we have placed homosexuality in our cultural church right now as the number one sin people can commit. That is the hot issue that we want to talk about and we want to deal with. My issue with the church is how militantly we have attacked homosexuality as a sin and how passively we go after the other sins in our culture. I want to dissociate myself from how the church has dealt with homosexuals—not that I think it's right to be a homosexual, but I think we have completely missed how we deal with it. We think we have to be militant and political and that somehow we are going to change all of society, instead of figuring out ways to minister to the homosexual.

DAD: I think it isn't being militant against homosexuals, but against the social and legal constraints that will come if that becomes the unquestioned moral standard.

 CHRIS: Now you're getting into a totally different conversation because I'm talking about Christian people. What Brian is saying is that if we are going to pick homosexuality out from all other sins, then we need to be really careful. So many people have gone on a rampage about homosexuality, and they hate people; there is no sense of love and compassion behind it. So now we as Christians are lumped in with them.

 DAD: Isn't that always the case? We don't want to be identified with the extremists of any group.

 CHRIS: Yeah, but Christian extremists are on TV constantly, and not just on TV—they are on every street. Go into any conservative fundamentalist church and what you get, essentially, is hatred. It's not the rare extremist; we are talking about the mainstream of fundamentalist Christians who are in that vein, and even when they try to temper themselves, the hate comes out.

SINNERS IN THE CHURCH

 ROBBIE: A few Sundays ago we had two lesbian women who come to our church sitting on the front row. And our biggest hope and prayer is that they actually join our community because we just don't feel like there is hope for them outside the community to ever realize the grace of God unless they get in with people who love them and nurture them. That is the most important thing to me—the way that we approach church membership and our association with them when it comes to repentance.

DAD: I guess it depends on what you mean by "join the community." I mean, it's one thing to be in relationship with the family, so that you might have a redemptive relationship. It's another thing to be publicly and officially identified as a believer, a professing believer. And if you accept them as professing believers when they are unrepentant in a sin that the Scripture says...

 ROBBIE: We would profess our public belief through baptism. That is our public profession of belief, and the way we view it is, "Please come join so that we can walk with you."

 DAD: I guess we would not use the word "join" because of the baggage. It may not have that baggage with you.

 ROBBIE: I just wonder if those people you talked about earlier left the church because they were not allowed membership, then.

 DAD: But membership...They were coming to be baptized. Are you going to baptize an unregenerate person? My plea to them was, "You know this is our stand, but hear me clearly, we love you. We want you to be a part." I know there are extremists, and the liberal media makes sure that they get the spotlight.

 CHRIS: But they are not just extremists, Dad. You could visit almost any Southern Baptist church, and you'd get the same hatred.

 PAPA: I disagree. I don't think that's true of all Southern Baptist churches.

 CHRIS: No, I'm not saying all, but I'm saying we are not talking about the fringe. I don't think it's everywhere, but it's still in the mainstream.

PAPA: Well, what's the difference? What if a couple comes down and they want to join the church and they are just living together—they are not married—do we accept them?

CHRIS: In the community, I think we do, yes.

DAD: Well, now we are getting into semantics. Would you baptize them if they were not repentant of their sin?

CHRIS: Probably not, no. But that's the challenge. It's like with all those things: we baptize unregenerate people every week.

DAD: I think it's just more difficult to say—are you guilty of adultery or are you guilty of gossip? If you are living together publicly in sin, it's easy to identify.

LEGISTLATING MORALITY

CHRIS: So, articulate the case for me. When people aren't people of faith, I don't think we should have any moral expectation for them. So then, why would the church spend so much time lobbying, giving money, and making it our mission to defeat these issues like gay marriage? What else could we expect from the culture?

DAD: Well, the issue is not to try to force them to act like Christians when they are not. The issue is the legal ramifications. For instance, in Canada they have just passed a law that any public speech that is deemed homophobic is punishable by imprisonment.

CHRIS: But that is a free speech issue. It doesn't have anything to do with gay marriage.

DAD: A pastor in Canada can legally be prosecuted if he stands in the pulpit and says that homosexuality is morally wrong.

 CHRIS: But that's a free speech issue.

 DAD: We are not trying to force homosexuals to act like Christians when they are not, and they are free to do as they choose.

 CHRIS: But it's the ACLU that would be up in arms about that. It's the people that the church tends to despise who would be the first ones to say that if the pastor is being prosecuted for that, we will pay your legal bills, we'll fight this thing. It doesn't have anything to do with gay marriage. The reality is that if you are not in faith, what you choose to do and your choice about gay marriage don't really have an effect on me. I mean, I know that what we want is to have a nation that is a better place; we want to be salt and light.

 DAD: I don't think you see the point. The whole issue of opposing gay marriage is not about hating homosexuals. It's not about trying to force them to do legally what they wouldn't do because of their heart. It's about the changes that would be eventually enforced on us legally if that became the accepted legal and moral norm of the nation.

 CHRIS: That's quite a leap, Dad, to say that it's going to be a totalitarian state where our speech isn't allowed.

 DAD: Have either of you read Dobson's book on the subject?

CHRIS: No, I don't read Dobson's books.

 DAD: Well, maybe you should have a more open mind and look at what he has to say.

 BRIAN: Well, honestly, how do you justify saying that we are fighting for free speech? I just don't see how you can make that leap from homosexual marriage to that. So what if we are persecuted? The early church was persecuted for the first 400 years and they did just fine. Why do we think we have to legislate America for us to be effective? Are we going to be a better church once we get the constitutional amendment passed? Or are we going to be a better church if we don't? I just don't see how it affects the church in such a grand way. Our calling is not to care if we are persecuted; it's to keep moving forward with being the church. I think this is just diverting attention away from being the real church, from being the salt and the light in the world. We are trying to delve into the personal lives of other people who aren't believers and trying to tell them what they can and can't do. It takes away from our focus of being the church.

 CHRIS: That's what it is, Dad: it's dictating the personal lives of people.

 DAD: They can do what they wish to do. It's about what we as a country are going to affirm.

 CHRIS: "We as a country" is different. That's different from "we as a church." As citizens, we can say, "Well, that's fine."

 DAD: I think we aren't going to solve our differences in this. It's a difference in perspective for what it means to be salt and light. I believe that also means you don't sit by and let the nation affirm the cultural and legal norms, saying that this is right and moral and if you disagree then you are liable for prosecution.

 CHRIS: You know that is not in the gay marriage amendment. You know none of that is in it—that you are going to be prosecuted if you say it's not right. In the bill that is coming before Congress no one has ever suggested pastors be prosecuted for saying things aren't right, but I don't know about this extreme case in Canada.

 DAD: It's not an extreme case; it is the law in Canada. Once homosexuality is viewed as the moral norm by the nation, it becomes the same kind of issue as hate speech against a person of a different race.

 CHRIS: We live in a nation with a great deal of tolerance for that.

 BRIAN: Hate speech is different. You can sit in here and say, "I don't like black people; I don't think they are good people," and you're not going to get arrested for it. But if you go find a black person and start threatening him with why you think he is a bad person, then you have moved from free speech to hate speech. It's not that you can't state an opinion anymore. I think homosexuality is wrong. That's not the issue for me. The issue for me is that if the church would embrace [the elimination of] poverty among young children with the same vigor they use to embrace the anti-homosexual marriage amendment, then we could do a lot of good for being salt and light in the world. But we *don't* embrace other issues because gay marriage is an issue we can be against without having to change anything in our own lives. We can use it as an issue and be against it and fight it because we never have to make a change—versus child poverty: we'd have to *do* something about that.

DAD: Oh, I agree.

 BRIAN: But the church as a whole—we've all failed, not just one side or the other. In not embracing these other issues—that is where we've lost sight.

 ROBBIE: Let me ask you two guys *(Chris and Brian)* this. Are you saying you would support the amendment, but you wouldn't waste our time as a church to go after that?

 BRIAN: No, I wouldn't support the amendment because I don't think it is our call to try to legislate morality on people who do not have the Holy Spirit in their lives.

 CHRIS: I think people actually find God faster while going down the degenerate path and coming to a place of emptiness—saying, "You know, what I really need is God and not all these other things." I think we try to make a happier and better world, but what we're going to end up with is a bunch of happier and more moral people in hell, which I think is a royal waste of time.

 DON MILLER: I think the conversation you guys are really having is about whether to be a missional church or not. The vigor with which people are attacking the issue of homosexuality is not the same vigor with which people attack divorce or extramarital affairs. It's completely different, but the issue is really the same: it's sin. So there is clearly one way—a missional mindset—where we care about what lost people think about us and about Christ and about Christians. And then the other way is where we care about morality and if lost people don't like us for it, that's fine—we don't care what they think. And so I think the real issue is motive. For a guy like Dobson—as good a person and a teacher as he is—I don't think he cares about whether homosexuals go to heaven or hell. I think he cares about building a utopia. He cares about building a Salt Lake City, Utah, but for Christians. I realize that sounds strong, but if he cared about whether homosexuals knew Christ, he would print tracts for homosexuals, not fight Congress. *Hmm.*

CHRIS: If he really cared about it, he would need to change the rhetoric a little bit. It's really hard to say you love these people that you speak ill of so often.

DAD: You are also forgetting the fact that he is very involved in a ministry of helping homosexuals come out of that lifestyle.

DON MILLER: In my opinion—and this is me judging him from a couple of weeks I spent with Dr. Dobson—that ministry is a token. I would bet he spends more effort on lobbying Congress than he does on converting gays. He has to throw a bone to some sort of conversion ministry in order to avoid the label. But his money is where his heart is, plain and simple. The only reason he is doing that is so he can say he's got this thing on the backburner, so you can't tell him he hates people. I don't think he really cares about the grace of Jesus as much as he does the morals of God. He will not speak against Mormonism because he is a moralist and they are moralists, too— they have this in common. I think Dobson uses the battle or war metaphor almost exclusively in dealing with these issues. I'm not saying he is a bad person and we should be against him; I'm saying his motive is morality and not the gospel. This, to me, is the difference between the two arguments: One wants people to know Christ. The other wants people to stop sinning and ruining our country.

DAD: I want to go back to what Brian said about having passion for other issues. I think part of the reason for the heightened awareness is the legislative dimension of it and what it takes to make a difference in the legislative arena. I agree that we need to have passion toward children's issues. This Saturday our church is doing a major outreach to children in our community, buying them backpacks and new shoes and immunizations and haircuts; and we do the mission trips. It's not that we don't believe in that—it's perhaps that it's not as visible. It's not an either/or; it's a both/and.

 BRIAN: I don't disagree that we do things. I just don't think that we as a church care as much about mobilizing people to do things in other areas. I mean, the mobilization of evangelicals against this particular amendment has been amazing. And we don't mobilize people the same way on other issues. To me, we are hook, line, and sinker on the bait of a political agenda, of a political season when both parties knew that this was a divisive issue. They both knew it would not be resolved, and they needed it to be talked about so there would be a line in the sand. In a lot of ways, the church has become the puppet of that political agenda. This is not to say that we aren't speaking truth about the issue, but we aren't being prophetic in any way. We're just being reactive to a political season, and we've become part of the political ploy.

 DAD: Well, I don't know that I would totally disagree with that, that there might be that kind of manipulation. I know you don't see it like this, so let me try to reframe it to help you understand the way that millions of American Christians see it.

 ROBBIE: And by the way, it's a 75-25 split in the general public—75 for this amendment, 25 against.

 BRIAN: It varies. I've seen two other statistics on that.

DAD: Here's how the passion is incited: if there were a movement in this country to once again legalize slavery, then obviously people of faith would be up in arms because they would see an incredibly dangerous and horrible change in the morals of our country. Obviously, that is not going to happen. That is a ridiculous hypothetical situation, but the same principles of the minds and understanding of these Christians apply. They see that if homosexuality becomes the legal and accepted moral norm, they see incredibly destructive long-term ramifications. I know that's not what you see.

 CHRIS: To compare an argument about justice and an argument about homosexual marriage is pretty ludicrous, though. To compare people being owned as property to people—who aren't people of faith—choosing to have a lifestyle that's different from what we would condone is crazy. If I were a black person I would be incredibly offended that you said that. Maybe to me that's just an illustration, but that's pretty over-the-top.

 DAD: It's an overstated principle. I'm trying to get you to see how evangelicals look at it as an incredibly dangerous path, morally and legally, for our nation.

 BRIAN: Dad, let me ask you this question. Take it out of America for a minute. What did the early church do when they had to deal with issues that were going on in their society like this? I mean, we could say the early church grew exponentially faster than anyone could ever have imagined, but they didn't believe they had to have the right circumstances going on around them to be effective as the church. Why is it that, post-Constantine, the only way we can be effective is to control society, to try to rein-in sin? I'm just confused as to where we left Scripture, and how we got to where we are, and why we think we have to create a perfect box for the church to be effective. Or is that a misstatement?

 DAD: No, it's not, and I think that's a valid question. But by that same logic, why was Chris so indignant because the church was silent during times of slavery?

 CHRIS: But justice is a different thing. Justice and oppression are not the same as moral choices made by free people.

 DAD: But the early church...

 CHRIS: The early church did not jump up and down and say, "You're immoral." Our commission is much more clear when it comes to issues of justice and mercy than it is for morality issues that don't actually harm and oppress people. I mean, homosexuality is not a good life for them, but ultimately, is that a gospel mandate? It is a clear gospel mandate to care for the poor and oppressed, but it never says to fight for personal morality. It's just a really different issue to me.

 DAD: Well, I just see it as a religious freedom issue and you don't, and I think we can just leave it at that. I think that's where the real difference of perspective lies, and only time will tell which one of us is right.

 BRIAN: I would say. So what if it's a religious freedom issue? The church has done just fine in places where there is no religious freedom, and maybe we would be a healthier church to be in one of those places. We have been so poisoned by being the majority.

 CHRIS: Brian said it really well. I think this is what Don is articulating about Dobson. I wish we knew if the church would do better in a place of oppression, in a place where the lines are more clear: either you're in the faith or you're not in the faith. You could say, "Man, the culture has really gone down the tubes, but the church is really healthy; the people have really defined who we are and what we believe, and we have become a strong missional church." I think people like Dobson would say they'd rather have a moral culture than have a strong church.

DAD: I think we're doing more judging of his motives than I'm comfortable with. I don't think we know what someone else's heart is, and I don't want anyone going and judging my heart. I think some incredible mistakes have been made when passion has led people to inappropriate expressions. I warned our church of this a long time ago when I first began to deal with this issue. It was in a dialogue forum on a Sunday night, and I had a crazy woman say she thought we ought to kill all the queers, and I had to lovingly but directly rebuke her and help her and the church understand that that is not what we are about. We are redemptive, and I said, "Let me make this crystal clear: we love all people because we are all sinners, and we are all condemned by sin, whether it is homosexuality or anything else. Sin is sin, and we are against sin but love the sinner. That does not mean we condone the sin."

ROBBIE: Maybe issues of justice are the times for us to really step in and campaign and use the government to make some change. It seems like abortion is something you guys would really jump all over because that is something we would obviously consider oppressive and unjust.

FOCUS ON THE GOSPEL

We often bemoan the decline of morality in our land as if we can expect something different from an increasingly post-Christian population. I am not an ambassador for morality, nor do I long to see the world become a more moral place. I want to see people come to faith in God, and only after they have come to faith will they see their entire lives transformed. We have made it very clear in our area of the city that we are not against homosexuality. Our mission is not to see people leave homosexual lifestyles, but for men and women to experience the freeing gospel of Jesus Christ. Hmm.

The church should refocus on the gospel instead of the culture wars. It is to our shame that we point out sin to our culture knowing that without the power of Christ, they are ill-equipped to change their lives. Instead, let us speak the love of Christ by loving all people. The apostle Paul made it very clear that you can do good things, even great things—but if you don't have love, it is useless. Jesus said, "Others will know you follow me if you love one another." A life of real faith is marked by love. The Bible says, "We love because he first loved us. If anyone says, 'I love God,' yet hates his brother, he is a liar. For anyone who does not love his brother, whom he has seen, cannot love God, whom he has not seen. And he has given us this command: Whoever loves God must also love his brother" (1 John 4:19-21).

CHAPTER 10

RACIAL ISSUES

How a Pastor Navigates the Color Divide

We sat at the table at Papa's house and all together we represented an enormous span of time. My grandfather was born in the 1920s, my father will live into the 30s of this century, and my brothers and I, God willing, will stretch out into the 2050s and 60s, leaving our children to find the next century. It is difficult to process how much change my grandfather has seen, how much of it my father noted in his youth, and how unlike the America they knew this new America has become.

One of the most dramatic shifts that's taken place during all the years represented at that table is the change in the racial divide. Certainly, racism still exists and it's an enormous, silent problem in the church. But it's not as profound as it was when my grandfather was entering into his calling as a pastor. Then it was profound, the earth was shaking with the shift. The white church, unfortunately, remained silent when their black brothers and sisters needed them. Silence is painful; we rarely live in the midst of silence because it makes us feel alone and reveals our fears and faults. Silence screams of indifference and disdain when it is offered in response to a need or injustice. There is perhaps no moment in Christ's life that is easier for us to identify with than his lonely walk to the cross, abandoned in silence by those who claimed to love him most.

Dr. Martin Luther King, Jr. and other civil rights leaders experienced a small part of that pain when the white church, whose voice would have given so much aid to the struggle for civil rights, failed to respond. It is often the church that takes the longest to change. When the Catholic Church admitted that Galileo was right after all—500 years too late—we laughed along with the late-night comedians, oblivious to the torturous struggles Galileo faced. As Methodists and Baptists have only recently apologized for their silence in the civil rights movement, we can only wonder at the pain our brothers felt in our silence and ignorance. To them, perhaps, it must have felt as though God himself was turning a deaf ear to their struggles.

Though it seems long ago for many of us too young to remember, it was only in 1955 that Rosa Parks refused to give up her bus seat. All these years later, the long road to civil rights is anything but history. We still struggle with integration, respect for cultural differences, and strained racial relations that may have scabbed over, but haven't truly healed.

The church has taken many steps, but there are still many more ahead. Throughout the following conversation, it quickly became evident that my grandfather's church, Mangum Oaks Baptist Church in Houston, was one of the first in Houston to see beyond the color of people's skin and look into their souls to find the image of God. My grandfather never got the memo about which terms are politically correct; he just knows the gospel has to transform our backward ideas.

SEGREGATION IN THE CHURCH

 ROBBIE: What was it like to be a pastor in the 1950s, 60s, and 70s when social issues were at the forefront of society? Was it hard to be in the pulpit when our ideas and laws relating to social issues were being changed?

 PAPA: When we were moving into this house, I found the minutes of a church meeting when desegregation happened. We saw that someone asked, "What are we going to do when someone brings a black baby into the nursery?" And the nursery worker in there said, "Well, I'll leave." And they argued for 30 minutes about whether or not to allow them, and finally, I remember, there was a little girl sitting next to Betty who stood up and said, "Well, if that ever happens, you call me and I'll hold the baby." Well, the consensus that night was that black people would not be accepted in the nursery or in the worship service.

DON MILLER: So they would be escorted out?

 CHRIS: So they weren't welcome?

 PAPA: That seemed to be what they were saying.

 DAD: I got chewed out back then by a deacon in East Texas because I let a little black boy on the bus, and that same deacon was there on Sunday night when a black teenager came and tried to go to the worship service. There were two First Baptist churches in Atlanta, Texas—a black one and a white one—and that old usher met that black boy in the foyer and said, "Boy, your church is over the hill."

 ROBBIE: That had a lot to do with you really wanting to leave, huh?

 DAD: I had a great relationship with the other First Baptist Church. It was so funny, though; the week after that happened we had a black kid on the bus, and that deacon chewed me out. He told me, "How could you let that n***** on our bus?" That next week we took the bus out and there were no white kids on the bus by the time I was finished. We had a busload of black kids and no sponsors except me. Nobody came, so I took them to the football game on the bus.

 CHRIS: Well, obviously all of this sounds ridiculous, but the fact that that old nursery worker was afraid of a black baby...

 PAPA: I think she was afraid it would come off.

CHRIS: Like it was a sickness.

PAPA: Yeah.

DAD: You have to understand, it was a different time. There was ignorance that people had not yet worked through.

PAPA: And you have to realize that they were raised like that. That's all she'd known her whole life: You don't sit with them, you don't sit by them, you don't eat with them, and you don't touch them.

DAD: That was the order of the society.

ROBBIE: The men who founded this country were God-fearing men, and they owned black people.

CHRIS: Doesn't that make you wonder how you can be Christian and really hear the voice of God?

DAD: There was a time that W.A. Criswell stood in the pulpit in First Baptist in Dallas and said, "It is God's will that the races be separated." What you have come to accept as normal and logical was not normal and logical back then.

CHRIS: Yeah, and I understand that all that was a part of the culture. I'm clearly immersed in the culture in so many ways, and part of what makes me unique and makes me Christian is that I have to question things in the culture. Hopefully the Holy Spirit is speaking to me when I think, "How is it that for so long no one was saying anything—in the church, at least?" I mean, most of the people in the civil rights movement came from black churches, and clearly there were some pastors and church leaders involved. But so many from the white churches weren't even talking about it. It makes you wonder: Did those people even know the real God?

 PAPA: Well, you see, it's biblical because Scripture says, "Birds of a feather flock together."

 BRIAN: Which book is that?

 PAPA: I don't know, but it's in there. You don't mix the races.

 DON MILLER: As we look back on the legacy of the church here in America, we see very beautiful stuff. I would just echo Chris's question about how the two co-existed. There is a legitimately beautiful story that's taking place: God is building a church, mission programs are unbelievable during this time, and yet there is this racism and prejudice. How could the Holy Spirit be moving in one aspect and just ignoring the other?

 PAPA: Well, you see, that's the idea. They said God didn't really work with the people whose skin is black, that they were cursed and God pushed them away and didn't want to have anything to do with them.

 CHRIS: But Pop, if they were uniquely Christian, don't you think somewhere along the way they would have heard the Spirit of God saying, "This is wrong and maybe Jesus was much closer to being black than white"?

 PAPA: Well, I think they did, but...

CHRIS: But they hardened their hearts.

 PAPA: Yeah. They pushed it away because they didn't want black people to be a part of their family. And so they moved away from that idea as fast as they could. You know, a friend of ours, if you asked him about the blacks, would say, "Yeah, I like the blacks. I think everyone ought to own one." And that's his idea still today. He doesn't want to have anything to do with it. My first real experience with blacks was in Mangum Oaks because that was where we had our first black deacon. Then we finally had about five or six; we had a mixture of white and black even in the early days.

 ROBBIE: When was this?

 PAPA: It probably started in the 80s.

 CHRIS: So there were just beginning to be multiracial churches then?

 PAPA: No, no. You couldn't say multiracial. Well, I guess you could.

 ROBBIE: There was a small percentage.

 PAPA: A very small percentage.

 CHRIS: But they were actually in leadership and had a voice and were trusted people in the church?

PAPA: Yeah.

 DAD: To answer your question, I think people get in denial. It's like many Christians are silent on the issue of abortion; they just don't want to deal with it. They know it's a problem and a sin and it's wrong, but they just don't want to be a part of confronting it.

 CHRIS: But it's a little easier to be passive about abortion and things that aren't right in your face. This is something you interacted with every day, right?

 DAD: Not really. They chose to separate themselves. They had as little contact and interaction as they could.

 CHRIS: If you saw a black man on the street and you chose not to interact or to sit in a separate place in a restaurant or bus, it was a conscious act to say, "I am going to sit in this place while they sit in that place."

 DAD: At that time, I remember my uncle taking me into a restaurant, and there were signs at every table that said "Reserved," and it was so black people could not sit there. In those days, you just didn't have any contact with them unless they worked for you. And that's just the way it was.

 PAPA: You know, then you had the wives cooking your meals and changing diapers and...

 BRIAN: Should the white church in America be ashamed of how slowly the church responded to the civil rights movement?

 DAD: Sure.

CHRIS: We didn't live then, but part of me wants to say we aren't going to see a lot of these people in heaven. I have a hard time fathoming that they really had a relationship with the living God.

 PAPA: We have a friend who gives a lot of money to missions, and I said, "Why do you do that?" He said, "To carry the gospel to them." Then I said, "Do you mean you are working in Africa with those people?" And he said, "Yeah." So I said, "Then how are you going to not care for them and try to move as far away from them as you can here, but say that one day you will live with them in heaven?" He said, "Oh, no, that won't be the case."

 CHRIS: Heaven is segregated? What you are saying is that you can be Christian and still have ideas that are not redeemed. You have allowed God to redeem some of you, but not all of you.

 DAD: Other people's sins are always more obvious than our own.

BLACK DEACONS

 DON MILLER: *(to Papa)* Now, Bob, you were pastor of a church, and you had on your deacon board at least five black deacons, is that right?

 PAPA: Yes.

 DON MILLER: Well, to be a white pastor and have black deacons is an anomaly nowadays, not just in the 80s. I don't know of any church that has black deacons that doesn't also have a black pastor.

DAD: We don't have any black deacons. We have very few black members.

 PAPA: Yes, we had five black deacons. One of them was not a good man, but that had nothing to do with his color.

 CHRIS: Which is a pretty typical ratio for deacons: you're going to have at least one bad deacon out of five. Your situation was probably much better, actually; it's probably usually more like 50 percent.

 DON MILLER: *(to Papa)* Did you initiate that, or did you step into that situation?

 CHRIS: How did it happen when you started to ordain black deacons?

 PAPA: We only ordained two black deacons; the rest came to us. We had a rule that no one could be in the deacon body until he had been there a year. I don't know that we had anybody—except a few in the congregation—that had anything to say against it when it came time for these to go on the deacon body. We didn't have anyone that voted against them. I think it was because we had tried to do our best over the months and the years to help everyone realize that there was no reason for segregation: that God loves the black and the white and the red and the green and the polka dotted, and whatever else may be. The time had come for us to accept God's will for our lives with these people, whether they were Negro or Mexican. We had to embrace a kingdom mindset. In the early 90s we had our first mixed race couple—we had a white girl and a black man. She was a missionary to Jamaica, and she married a Jamaican. And we had another couple—she was Mexican and he was black. Over the years our people began to accept that and believe that this was the right thing for us to do.

DON MILLER: That process began as you led from the pulpit. Well before you had a multiethnic church, you prepared their hearts for fellowship with people of other races. I wish more pastors had led their churches through these issues.

 CHRIS: What would have been the perception if you had quoted MLK, Jr. in a sermon?

 PAPA: I did. Of course every preacher somewhere down the line has quoted, "We are free, free at last," and there were a few other things. I think in the early years we had a good group of great Christians. I think if I had tried to lead them in any other direction, I wouldn't have lasted there. The majority would have said, "This is not the way to go because the Bible tells us to love, and that's what we're going to do."

 DAD: There's a huge difference in the attitudes of churches in suburban Houston and Dallas as opposed to, say, deep east Texas. The church I served in may be a little more multiracial today, but not much.

INTERRACIAL MARRIAGE

 CHRIS: Your church was an urban church. It was a melting pot around the church, but not in the church. This conversation describes a lot of change, though: going from the minutes of a business meeting where they wouldn't take a black baby in the nursery to leading your church to really integrate, and now you have an African-American grandson. That is an unbelievable amount of change in your lifetime.

 PAPA: Yeah, I would say that is a change. It's an acceptable thing now to marry interracially.

DAD: Did you ever have parents try to get you to tell their son or daughter that it was unbiblical? How did you handle that?

PAPA: I told them it was up to them as parents to raise their children. I said, "You'll have to show me where that is, biblically." I'm not saying I was in favor of that, but I was saying I wouldn't have anything to do with it.

ROBBIE: Dad, do you get that a lot?

DAD: I wouldn't say a lot. I've had it a couple of times through the years, and what I say to them is, "There may be reasons that you are uncomfortable with this. There may be reasons why you think it's wrong, but you are not going to be able to justify that in Scripture. Don't look for something that's not there."

BRIAN: They try to go with "unequally yoked."

DAD: Yeah, and you know, I told them that's not even it.

CHRIS: But you have to know, I was going through [the book of] Numbers last week and it says that Miriam and Aaron were speaking against Moses because of his Cushite wife. She was Ethiopian: literally it means she had dark skin. Now we don't know what they were bothered about—probably her culture. And then God spoke to Moses face to face, and God forgot to mention it if he didn't like it.

DAD: You confront your own struggle with that when you get a daughter of dating age. You ask yourself how you're really going to feel if she brings home someone of a totally different culture. Mom and I came to the conclusion that if it was a good Christian boy who loved the Lord and had good character and integrity, then we would be more comfortable with that than a white boy who had none of those things. You think you know until your daughter is that age.

BRIAN: But my generation didn't grow up with quite the disdain that you guys were raised on, so I think it's easier for us to say we will be okay with it. The racial issue isn't as strong as it was in the influence of your life. You were taught that black people were one way and white people were another way. But we were taught that we are all created in the image of God, no matter the color of our skin. So I think I can say with sincerity that I don't think it will be as much of an issue with my generation.

CHRIS: As a pastor, it would be a great thing to be involved in an interracial marriage because you would make so many more connections. I am so thankful God gave me the wife he gave me, but in some ways having a spouse of a different race would be much better in terms of building bridges.

GRANDMA: THE RACIST

DAD: Now, your great-grandmother, who was a wonderful godly woman, loved the Lord with all her heart. And she had a black woman she loved who worked for her for years. But it was so ingrained in her, [the belief] that "there's nothing wrong with n*****s as long as they stay in their place." And to her, there was no inconsistency. She just grew up with that being the accepted norm, and that is so foreign to us.

DAD: In her mind there was absolutely no malice. She was probably the most loving person.

CHRIS: She probably heard it from the pulpit, and—God rest her soul—it is still disgusting and wrong.

 BRIAN: Well, yeah, it was the cultural norm, but it makes it no less wrong.

 CHRIS: You have to wonder about the place where the church is now. How much of it is a result of the sins of the church over the past 100 years?

 BRIAN: It also makes me wonder which cultural norms, which statements, which issues are we just accepting as the church? We just swallow them and say, "Oh well, that's just who we are." The church should be more prophetic. When the rest of the church in the 1940s and 50s was saying, "Oh, it's okay. We just trust the government," Bonhoeffer and the professing church in Germany said, "No, we don't. That's not right. We are going to stand up to that." There are still those minority voices. I'm just curious as to what those issues are today. Are we aware of them? The Sudan, the World Bank—do we take a stand against injustice in the world? As great as America is, don't we need to take a stand for the little mice that the elephant keeps stepping on?

 DAD: They are so much clearer in retrospect. You can't see them easily when you're right in it.

 BRIAN: We are also in a democracy where the majority rules, and so we don't like to listen to the minority voices.

WALK ALONG THE NARROW ROAD

I have to be honest: this dialogue is painful for me to read. When I hear my Dad describe his grandmother (a woman who selflessly raised him) as a good Christian and a racist, I want to puke. Can you be both? My short answer is *no*; but I can be prideful and consumed by many other sins, and I don't doubt the grace that is offered to me through Christ. I sound like a jerk even raising the possibility that my "sweet granny" is in hell. What kind of great-grandson am I? The reality is that all cultures are broken, sick, unregenerate, and depraved. Which is worse: slavery and prejudice, or the sexual revolution and rampant drug addiction? None of it is what we are made for. If we lose sight of the kingdom we are seeking and become complacent, hope is lost. Christ is redeeming all cultures, creations, and relationships.

Sins of omission surround us each day when we fail to act, to seek justice, to respond, and to pray; we sin by our silence and indifference. The church, historically slow to react to injustice but quick to bend to popular opinion, must no longer live in neglect. The narrow road we are called to travel often directs us to walk beside those who are alone and to become a voice for those whose cries are being drowned out. The gospel is all about the marginalized minority.

I am inspired, too, by my father and grandfather. My father, who took a busload of black children to a football game by himself, stood up to his own church. My grandfather recruited black deacons in a place that only a few years before wanted to ignore a black baby. And I have to stand in my pulpit and say to the beautiful and wonderful people I shepherd, "There is a world outside our country. Our brothers and sisters in Africa, in India, in the Sahara, are calling to us. We have to talk to them; we have to ask them what they need." My brother Brian is right; this is the sin of the church today—my church and your church. This is our movement. This is our revolution. God forgive our neglect. May we return to the true gospel of Jesus Christ, and may God forgive me, as he has forgiven my granny.

CHAPTER 11

TO BE ME OR NOT TO BE ME?

How a Pastor Navigates
Authenticity and Vulnerability

In ministry, this is the ultimate question: *Will I live my life hiding my thoughts, fears, sins, and insecurities; or will I expose the world to my humanity?* If people see my rough edges, will they still respect me as their pastor; or will they reject me for not meeting their expectations?

It's remarkable to me that while living in a world that's inhabited by 6 billion other human beings, each of us can still feel as though our experience is unique. Our theology teaches the universal brokenness of humanity, but each of us—alone at night, driving in the car, walking in the rain, sitting on an airplane—feels that he is the only broken person, the only one whose wiring is defunct. In this way, the open person—the disclosing pastor—has a power to speak into the deepest question of the human soul: *Am I alone in my weakness?* The community of Christ, then, becomes a refuge: we are not alone at being human.

In my life there has been a certain ache. I've spent some time walking in the rain, some time sitting in an airplane, some time wondering if I were the only broken human. I shove my stories into bottles and cast them from a vacant shore, always relieved to find, as Sting has said, a hundred million bottles returned the next morning—a sign that *I am not alone at being alone*.

TAINTED HISTORY

By now you know my family. We are leaders. We stand behind pulpits and translate God. Are we still qualified to lead and speak if we have secrets? Is the messenger a part of the message? Can ancient, otherworldly, perfect, and beautiful truths be entrusted to broken humans? I suppose the binary question would be, *To whom else might it be entrusted?*

Our story, the story of my family, is a broken story. I have always sensed a hidden wound in our story, something that we couldn't talk about. I've never found the scars to prove the injury, but I sensed that my hunch was correct. I've never artic-ulated it until now. My fingers are trembling at the keyboard, as I fear the other people in this book will be angry with me for speaking up. I'll just say it: I always believed I was illegitimate. You know, a bastard.

At age four I remember thinking there was something wrong with the timing surrounding my birth. I was unexpected, and my arrival put everyone on eggshells and made problems. Upon further investigation, I discovered there were eleven months separating my parents' wedding date and my birth, but it made me feel no better.

My gut told me there were secrets surrounding my parents' wedding and my birth, and the secrets created an internal shame. It was as if I'd done something wrong. Even now I know that by talking about it I have crossed a line; my mother will be angry, hurt, or embarrassed by the telling of this story. But it is my story, too, and it is the *secret* that hurts me, not the truth. The secret creates a space for shame and unknow-ing. The strange consequence of hiding the past is that those around us begin to imagine circumstances that are worse than the truth.

When any of my siblings are brave enough to broach the sub-ject of the strange conditions of my parents' nuptials in a query, comment, or joke, the backlash is immediate. We have learned to leave the subject alone—the events surrounding my parents' wedding are a secret!

Like all secrets, they lie under the surface peeking through at every opportunity. It's clear my grandfather hasn't forgotten. When we talked about the difficulties of his life and ministry, one circumstance repeatedly came to light.

PAPA: In Mangum Oaks there were difficulties with some staff members. I had a music director *(Dad)* I had to dispose of. He tried to make some flak.

 BRIAN: Way to go, Dad.

 PAPA: Well, we called a man to be the minister of music, and he was also the youth minister. One of the things we told him was, "You don't date any of the youth."

 DAD: Now, you're not telling that story right. I asked if that was a policy, and you said, "Well, that's not really necessary."

 PAPA: Well, that was a policy...and he married her.

 DAD: I didn't date her; I just married her.

A SECRET LOVE

The tension in the room was still palpable, all these years later. Something happened in my father's courtship of my mother. This was big, and 33 years have not erased the tension. And of course, I sat there with my silent questions.

My dad is a play-by-the-rules kind of guy. You can count on him to do the right thing. I've always wondered where this came from; he didn't have a father present to teach him how to be a man. His grandmother raised him in a loving Christian home where his mother seemed more like an aunt. Most kids who experience the early death of a father and who grow up with an alcoholic (although absent) mother are on the fast track to prison, not Christian ministry. So, how did my father become the kind of man who doesn't break the rules? This is how straight and narrow my father is: In 1989, Dad went out on a financial limb and bought a Chevy Astro Van. This was a logical purchase for a family of seven, but finances were tight. So we financed it over four years hoping the already used vehicle could outlast the payments. After one year of making payments, GM Financial Services sent Dad a congratulatory note for paying off the vehicle and a free and clear title. There was only one problem: we hadn't paid it off. I called it grace from God. But my father called GM and spent hours on the phone trying to convince them that they'd made a mistake and should accept his monthly payments for the next three years. Their records said PAID IN FULL, and they couldn't figure out why this persistent pastor would argue the matter. Keeping the title was never an option; it wasn't right.

So what had my father done that deserved such secrecy? What did he do that nobody would talk about? The truth began to surface when we came together to begin discussions about this book. Our inquiry into the truth was unwelcome and accompanied by the requisite disclaimer—*If your mom knew I was telling you this...*The words that followed portrayed a different scenario from anything we had imagined. If it were a play, it would have three acts:

> Act 1: My father, 20 years old and driving a 1968 Ford Mustang, takes a job as minister of music and youth at my grandfather's church. In the choir is a beautiful, blond 16-year-old vocal and piano prodigy, and his interests quickly go beyond choral music to romance. This is a forbidden love, according to the employee policy manual, but it is mutual and undeniable.

> Act 2: This romance can't stay a secret, the couple decides. It consumes them. If they confess their love for each other, everyone will understand and her father will offer his blessing on the marriage despite her young age. But instead of

blessings, my grandfather denies their request. Marriage is not an option.

Act 3: Love must die or find a way. So, filled with youthful passion like Romeo and Juliet, my parents find a way. They move forward with plans to marry secretly. And my father's new young wife continues to live in her childhood home with my grandfather. That's when I arrived on the scene, and the whole thing shook down like that tragic day in the Garden of Eden. My father's secret wife was pregnant!

My father told us this story with a great deal of shame in his voice; but to my brothers and me, it sounded wildly romantic. Romance dwarfed reality. The truth is that my dad did not start off on the right foot with his new family. Foolish? No doubt about it. But was it worth the years of secrecy and shame? No.

Why not be honest? Why not be human? I'm not an illegitimate child. I'm just a man who took on unnecessary shame while growing up. My parents have no reason to hold onto any guilt from 30 years ago—they were two young people who were passionately in love. What they did seems romantic and idealistic (in the best sense of the word) to their children. I know my parents in a different way now, and regardless of the great job they did raising us, this secret created a distance between us. That's what secrets do. Now I begin that journey of forgiveness and celebration with the people who brought me into this world. I love them more than words can say and I respect them more each day.

Is the answer to live your life as an open book, broadcasting your failures to friends and enemies alike? No. There should be different levels of disclosure with family, close friends, small group, church, and the public. But you must disclose, or you will be relegated to the world of stick figures or worse—put on a pedestal.

Christ alone was perfect. Though you may strive to be holy as he is holy, you will not achieve it. Reveal your struggles to those who journey with you; they are snapshots of redemption. The same tension that my parents brought into my inner life might also be instilled in the inner life of your congregation, creating a community of people who are all playing make-believe. Why not cast a bottle into the ocean and give your congregation the freedom to cast bottles back, thus allowing a community of humans to no longer feel alone?

I have always had trouble getting up in the morning. In high school my dad would drag me to the shower and turn it on, only to come back and find me huddled under the streams of water and dreaming that I was drowning. Like every pastor, my ultimate nightmare is that everyone will arrive at church except for me. One week I woke up late and ran to the shower. I kicked the metal bed frame on my way to the bathroom, which caused my big toe to erupt with blood from under the toenail. This hurt badly—really badly—and I expressed my displeasure with very colorful language. Later that morning during the sermon—as I explained my new, subtle limp—I confessed to a couple of four-letter words that came forth in the heat of the moment. Some were scandalized by my honesty, but to the majority I became a real person that day. Other than Mother Teresa, there are only two people on the planet who do not cuss when they extract a toenail. If you are more like Mother Teresa than most people, I give you my respect; but if you are more like the rest of us, don't feel compelled to lie about it.

Fifty years ago, a good religious system was merited by its ability to create a great (read: moral) human, but this isn't so true anymore. Today, a religious system is measured by its ability to make honest humans: people who can look at them-selves in the mirror and then walk away, not forgetting who they really are.

DISCUSSION QUESTIONS

CH. 1—SOME INTRODUCTIONS

1. What is the legacy you've received from previous generations?

2. What kind of legacy do you want to pass down to your children and to your grandchildren?

CH. 2—SOME THINGS JUST CHANGE

1. What kinds of cultural divides do you deal with in your congregations?

2. What can we learn from those older Christians who have been in the faith their whole lives?

3. Our outlooks are inevitably going to be different than the outlooks of those who were raised 50 years before us, but how can we find ways to compromise?

CH. 3—THE INNER LIFE

1. Think about your darkest times in ministry. What could have helped you in those times? Time off? Talking with friends in the ministry?

2. Are you afraid at times to admit your struggles and show your fatigue in ministry? Why?

CH. 4—FAMILY

1. In what ways is childrearing different for a pastor than for any other Christian parent? How can a pastor deal with the "Glass House Syndrome"?

2. In what ways do Paul's hypothetical questions in Galatians 1:10 ("Am I now trying to win the approval of men, or of God? Or am I trying to please men?") apply to a pastor who becomes more concerned with "image management" than with the spiritual nurture of his own children?

3. How have you neglected your wife and kids because of ministry? Go ask them.

4. In what ways can you guard the time spent with your family from the demands of a priority crisis?

CH. 5—A STUDY IN POWER

1. Are you able to articulate the basic theological essentials of Christianity? Is that important?

2. There are factual discrepancies in Scripture; does that in any way affect its authority and the way we read it?

CH. 6—WHEN I REALIZED PASTORS ARE SOMETIMES ARROGANT JERKS

1. How can Christians—even pastors—who are members of the body of Christ, act in ways that are so un-Christlike? How can you keep from falling into that trap?

2. How can you deal redemptively with people who attack you unfairly and act so petty toward you?

3. How can you go about forgiving those people?

4. What can you do to make certain that you keep your eyes on God and not on his cynical and confused children?

CH. 7—GOVERNMENT AND POLITICS

1. What role should a pastor play concerning the topic of politics in your congregation?

2. What does it really mean for us to be pro-life?

3. Is there an adequate Christian response to abortion?

4. When does life begin?

5. Is legislating abortion appropriate or feasible?

6. How do I teach my congregation about the sanctity of human life?

7. How do I teach people that an African life is as important as the life of a newborn child?

CH. 8—HOW TO MAKE MILLIONS OFF JESUS

1. In what ways have you seen God bless you and your family for your stewardship?

2. Stewardship is more than just giving to the church; it also involves using what we have the right way. How do you convey that message to a congregation with words and with actions?

CH. 9—SOCIAL ISSUES

1. Should Christians remain silent in the moral debates of the secular culture? If not, how do we speak redemptively?

2. How can we communicate unconditional love toward any unbeliever who is caught in the futility of sin, but without leaving a mistaken impression that we are affirming their sin?

3. How do we call someone to repentance from sin and to redemption in Christ without seeming judgmental or condemning?

4. For you, what does it mean to be salt and light when relating to the homosexuality issue?

5. How do we welcome homosexuals into the church?

CH. 10—RACIAL ISSUES

1. Just as earlier generations of Christians had a "blind spot" in the area of racial equality, what could some of the possible "blind spots" be for today's generation of believers in the area of justice and equality issues?

2. How do you balance gender differences and cultural distinctives with the equality that Paul spoke of in Galatians 3:28— "There is neither Jew nor Greek, slave nor free, male nor female, for you are all one in Christ Jesus"?

3. The author wrote that church is "still the most segregated place in America." How do we change that? Should we even try to?

CH. 11—TO BE ME OR NOT TO BE ME

1. At times are you afraid to have your faults known? Is that a legitimate fear?

2. What secrets (your own or others') hover over your life? Can being honest about them help you to overcome them?

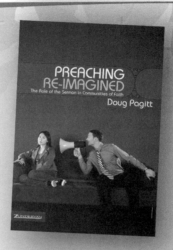

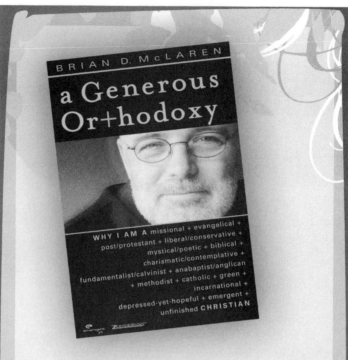
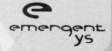

In a conversational narrative style, author Dan Kimball guides church leaders on how to create alternative services from start to finish. He explains why youth pastors are usually the ideal staff to start a new service.

Emerging Worship
Creating Worship Gatherings
for New Generations
Dan Kimball

RETAIL $14.99
ISBN 0310256445

Today's postmodern generation does not respond to church like the generations before them. Author Dan Kimball explains the implications of the postmodern shift for the church and provideds practical ideas on how it can use worship, preaching, evangelism, discipleship, and leadership to reach emerging generations.

The Emerging Church
Vintage Christianity for new generations
Dan Kimball

RETAIL $16.99
ISBN 0310245648

emergent
ys

Visit **www.emergentys.com**
or your local Christian bookstore.

What's going on out there?

Steve Taylor tells us what he's finding inside the emerging church around the world. From the revival of ancient practices to the rise of multimedia, he posts messages to us about worldwide church culture and sketches a view of the body of Christ at the borders. Whether you're inside or outside the emerging culture, this book will provide an intimate look at the far-flung areas of the church and present a scenario of what's to come.

The Search to Belong is a practical guide for pastors and church leaders—in fact, all leaders—who struggle with building community in a culture that values belonging over believing.

"A simple insight (your true 'belongings' are not your possessions, but the people to whom you belong and who belong to you) leads Joseph R. Myers to some of the most revolutionary and original thinking about small groups in the church today."

-Leonard Sweet, Drew Theological School, George Fox University, preachingplus.com

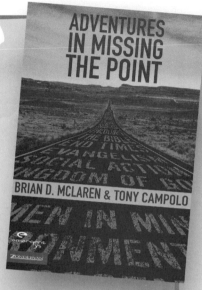

Join this exploration of exactly how we're missing the point regarding hot topics such as salvation, the Bible, postmodernism, justice, and leadership—and what we're supposed to be about. *Adventures in Missing the Point* isn't about pointing fingers at "them" for their mistakes. It's about us. Professionals and lay-workers, Protestants and Catholics, liberals and conservatives, Pentecostals and Presbyterians—all of us, trying to wake up to new possibilities for the Christian church in the postmodern world.

Ad enwres in Missing vhe Poinv
How the Culture-Controlled Church Neutered the Gospel
Brian McLaren, Tony Campolo

RETAIL $16.99
ISBN 0310267137

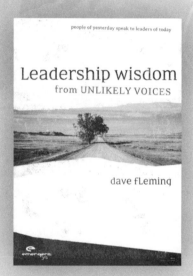

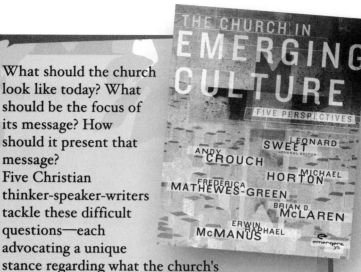

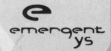